THE TOP
100
International
TEA
R E C I P E S

D1284458

THE TOP 100 International TEA
R E C I P E S

How to prepare, serve and experience great cups of tasty, healthy tea and tea desserts

M A R Y   W A R D

Lifetime Books, Inc.
Hollywood, Florida
800-771-3355
http: www//lifetimebooks.com
e-mail: lifetime@shadow.net

Prop/food stylist: Mary Ward
Book Designer/Art director: Donna Jean Morris
Photographer: Barney Taxel
Introduction: Timothy J. Castle
Typesetting/Layout: Vicki Heil

To order additional copies of *The Top 100 International Tea Recipes*, please send a check or money order for $14.95 (plus $3.00 shipping/handling) to: Lifetime Books, Inc. 2131 Hollywood Blvd., Hollywood, FL 33020. Please write to us to receive a free catalog and information on upcoming books that interest you.

Library of Congress Cataloging-in-Publication Data
Ward, Mary, 1940-
    The top 100 international tea recipes / by Mary Ward.
        p. cm.
    Includes bibliographical references and index.
    ISBN 0-8119-0817-8 (pbk.)
    1. Tea. 2. Cookery (Tea) 3. Tea--History. I. Title.
  TX817.T3W37   1996
  641.6'372--dc20   96-27101
                                       CIP

Other Books by Mary Ward:
THE TOP 100 INTERNATIONAL COFFEE RECIPES (1996)
THE TOP 100 COFFEE RECIPES (1992)
DR. ART ULENE'S LOW FAT COOKBOOK, Recipes by Mary Ward (1995, 1996)
DR. ART ULENE'S LUCIOUS, LOW FAT DESSERTS, Recipes by Mary Ward (1996)
BLUE RIBBON BREADS with Carol Stine (1988, 1996)
COUNT OUT CHOLESTEROL COOKBOOK with Dr. Art Ulene (1988, 1990, 1992)
THE OAT BRAN COOKBOOK (1988, 1989)

TABLE OF CONTENTS

Photos by Barney Taxel

Design by Donna Morris

INTRODUCTION

*T*his book is about celebrations . . . celebration of life, celebration of some of the great ceremonies of life, and about celebrating the benefits and pleasures of drinking tea. As author and reader, we will together discover the unlimited possibilities of brewing and drinking tea. Through the expertise of our tea artist, Daniel Mantey, we'll keep records and discover how to draw unbelievable flavors from the teas we brew.

*T*hen, as author, I'll take you on a culinary adventure . . . studying and sampling some traditional and international recipes for tea as a beverage . . . be it hot, iced, herb or spirited. Once your feet are "wet," you and I will move into the "meat" of this book . . . how to throw a great tea celebration.

*A*s author and home economist, I've tried to pull all the stops and include recipes for tea and goodies that are memorable and delicious, as well as easy to prepare. As author and hostess, I'll share tips for setting up a great tea tray . . . with suggestions for preparing several different types. You stand to benefit from some of the most memorable experiences of my life . . . taking tea with a friend.

The reader will discover that the English style of steeping tea is relatively new. As author and historian, I'll draw a verbal time line dating 5000 years ago to 3000 BCE (Before the Common Era), and Daniel will show a physical time line of the same. Through the very authentic and beautiful photography of Barney Taxel, photographic illustrator, and Donna Morris, art director, the reader will be able to picture the authenticity of both Chinese and Japanese Tea Ceremonies.

It makes sense that Westerners are eager to discover the tastes of tea. Probably the one thing most responsible for tea's popularity is its ability to transform itself through the various procedures of brewing. In Chapter 2, Daniel will teach not only the basics of brewing a memorable cup of tea, but will also give the reader a list of proper tea utensils while moving into the two-pot tea brewing method. Daniel's hope is that readers everywhere will start buying tea pots and experimenting with all types of teas. In fact, Daniel conducts a tea tasting each Sunday at his store, The Wabi Shop, in the Murray Hill district of Cleveland, Ohio. On a usual Sunday, Daniel might be conducting a tasting of various Taiwanese teas, perhaps tastes of hand-picked Japanese teas, or even tastes of $300-a-pound Prize First Flush Darjeeling.

Internationally, traditions of brewing and flavoring teas are of historic value and date back to 3000 BCE when tea was consumed as a soup. In Japan, the drinking of Mat-cha (thick, green, whipped tea) dates to the beginning of the Common Era. More recently, Russians prepare their tea in a Samovar and the Sri Lankans prepare theirs strong and extremely hot. The Indians enjoy cardamom in their beverage while Aussie's prepare their tea in a "Billy." Chapter 3 will explore the international options in easy-to-understand recipes which include international measurements.

I understand that there are purists who would argue that tea should be consumed hot, black and unsweetened. I love tea and its gregarious nature too much to allow these purists to lead such a dismal experience. Together, we'll explore the options of using tea with herbs, spices and a variety of other ingredients.

It is this author's pleasure to lead the reader to explore herbal teas, medicinal teas, iced teas and teas with spirits. Additionally, I'll challenge the reader to enjoy tea with honored guests in an Afternoon Tea Party . . . with children or grandchildren in a Nursery Tea Party . . . with family at an English Breakfast Tea and with dear friends in a Japanese Tea Party. All tea parties are illustrated photographically.

As in all my cookbooks, I feel a responsibility to analyze all recipes for calories, percentage calories from fat, saturated fat, cholesterol, sodium, caffeine and where applicable, percentage calories fat from alcohol. Where indicated, low fat products may be substituted for those with a higher fat content.

I also understand that many people are not born with culinary skills. With this in mind, easy as well as more challenging recipes are presented in Chapters 6 and 7. The author as well as graphic artist Donna Morris, have tried to write these recipes in an easy-to-read style. These are personal favorite recipes . . . well tested as well as delicious.

It is my hope this book will become a first step into the discovery of the wonderful world of tea drinking. May this exploration fill your life with meaning, good health and the love of good friends.

Author, Mary Ward

A STATEMENT FROM LIFETIME BOOKS

The Top 100 International Tea Recipes shows you how to prepare, serve and experience great cups of tasty, healthy tea, and tea desserts. It is a celebration of original and classic tea recipes. With full-color photographs (the perfect gift) and step-by-step instruction, you learn the secrets to making the perfect cup of hot or iced tea!

The *New York Times* once pronounced "tea is becoming the coffee of the 90's." Indeed, tea is as popular as ever around the world. Author Mary Ward searched the globe and is proud to present her finest recipes for your pleasure.

Now you can experience the joy of tea. Mary Ward pays homage to this time-honored, almost universal tradition. Warm your body, soothe your taste buds and sit back with a nice cup of tea. Here is a tribute to the elegant ritual of "taking tea."

Tea is the chinese cure for ills and an English mealtime institution. Whether we consume tea to heal our pain or enhance our pleasure, we can all appreciate the virtues of tea. You will learn how to choose the right tea for the right occasion. Each menu provides suggestions for the ideal tea to suit the meal. As a result, you will get cozy and intimate with others through tea.

The Top 100 International Tea Recipes is part of our new cookbook series that includes the companion book, *The Top 100 International Coffee Recipes*, also by Mary Ward. For more information on Lifetime Books' cookbooks, please contact us at 1-800-771-3355 or consult your favorite bookstore. Enjoy!

—Senior Editor
Brian Feinblum

*I'd like to dedicate this book
to the current and future tea drinkers of the world.*

*Without the following individuals this book would not have become
reality: Daniel Mantey, Donna Morris,
Barney Taxel, Don and Barbara Lessne,
Brian Feinblum, and Vicki Heil.*

Most especially, a thanks to the patience of my family.

Mary Ward

1 TEA: A ROMANTIC MOMENT IN TIME

A *while back, Don Lessne, who is a longtime friend and publisher of Lifetime Books, invited me to write a tea book. As he envisioned it, the work was "a natural" for a couple of reasons, since it followed our successful book,* The Top 100 International Coffee Recipes. *For one, this beautiful little book, paired with the newly revised coffee book, would make quite a set. For another, the timing is right since tea is increasingly being termed the next beverage boom.*

I *have to confess I didn't know that much about tea except that I love its taste and the way people drink it. I love tea parties and celebrations. I have attended and hosted "high teas" (although in the course of writing the book I learned that the proper terminology is "afternoon tea") and "breakfast tea." And soon, when I've moved into my new townhouse with its Japanese garden, I'll be entertaining with Japanese tea celebrations. As a grandmother, I have tea sets in all sizes and shapes. Melanie and Laura, my two granddaughters, love to have tea while we play with doll houses and Barbies and all the other things grandmothers and little girls love to share.*

So, after speaking with Don I went to the library, to the the bookstore and to the internet to find out what I could about tea. And for the last few months I have read, re-read and studied tea (in addition to drinking quite a lot of it). Probably the most interesting insight I've learned is that despite our familiarity with the stuff, we Westerners are really novices at drinking tea.

The history of tea goes back to 2737 BCE. (For reading purposes: BCE refers to "Before Common Era", before year 1. CE refers to "Common Era", after year 1.) It was then, according to legend, that tea was first used in China during the reign of Emperor Shen Nung. Included as a primary ingredient in soups and stews, Emperor Nung seems to have played a role in developing and passing on agricultural methods vital to tea. There is also evidence that peoples in Thailand and Myanmar have used tea for as long as the Chinese. But the plant would remain in the Orient for the next 3,500 years.

Look at this time line:

Hsia Dynasty, c. 1994-1523 BCE
Semi-legendary Emperor Yu built irrigation channels, reclaimed land. Bronze weapons, chariiots, domestic animals used. Wheat, millet cultivated. First use of written symbols.

Shang or Yin Dynasty, c. 1523-1027 BCE
First historic dynasty. Complex agricultural society designed to grow the tea plant. Well-developed writing and production of the first Chinese calendar. Bronze metallurgy.

Chou Dynasty, c. 1027-256 BCE
Classical age (Confucius, Lao-Tze, Mencius) despite turbulence.

Ch'in Dynasty, c. 256-202 BCE
China unified under the harsh rule of Shih Huang-ti. Feudalism replaced by centralized imperialism. Great Wall begun.

Han Dynasty, c. 202 BCE-220 CE
Imperial age, notable for its long and peaceful rule, expansion of territories, and technical and artistic involvement.

Three Kingdoms, c. 220-265 CE
Division into three states: Wei, Shu, Wu. Wei gradually dominant. Confucianism eclipsed; increased importance of Taoism and Buddhism.

Tsin or Chin Dynasty, c. 265-420 CE
Founded by a Wei general; gradual expansion of the southeast. Series of barbarian dynasties ruled North China. Continued growth of Buddhism.

Sui Dynasty, c. 420-618 CE
Reunification; centralized government reestablished, Buddhism, Taoism favored. Great Wall refortified; canal system established.

T'ang Dynasty, c. 618-906 CE
Glorious territorial expansion reaching from Korea to Turkistan. Age of great achievements in poetry, sculpture, painting.

Japanese Tea, c. 800 CE
The camellia (tea) plant is exported to Japan and used as a medicine.

Five Dynasties and Ten Kingdoms, c. 907-960 CE
Period of warfare, official corruption, general

hardship. Widespread development of paper money first printed.

Sung Dynasty, c. 960-1260 CE
Scholarly studies and artistic progress marked by the invention of moveable type.

Chinese Tea Ceremonies, c. 1300 CE
The oldest tea ritual begins.

Yuan Dynasty, c. 1260-1368 CE
Mongol dynasty founded by Kublai Khan. Growing contact with West, Confucian ideals and a visit from Marco Polo.

Ming Dynasty, c. 1368-1644 CE
Mongols expelled. Confucianism, civil service examinations reinstated. Contact with European traders, missionaries. Porcelain, architecture, the novel and drama flourish.

Japanese Tea Ceremony, c. 1500 CE
Senno Rikyu formulates rules of the cermony.

European Introduction, c. 1610 CE
Water route established methods of forward

transporting tea to Europe. By the end of the century, Tea Houses were being built throughout Europe.

Introduction to the U.S., c. 1670 CE forward
Tea did not arrive in the Americas until the latter part of the seventeenth century, around 1670. It did not come with instructions...and some colonists found more unusual ways to consume it. For example, in Salem, Massachusetts, the colonists boiled tea leaves until bitter, drank the liquid tea without sugar and consumed the tea leaves with salt and butter.

Russian Introduction, c. 1700 CE forward
Land routes from Tibet introduce the first teas to Russia.

Ch'ing or Manchu Dynasty, c. 1644-1912 CE
Established by the Manchus. Territorial expansion but gradual weakening of Chinese power; decline of central authority. Increasing European trade; foreign powers divide China into spheres of influence.

English Breakfast Tea

Start the day with this lovely tea celebration. Use the most beautiful teapot available teemed with creamy chicken over Belgian waffles, crunchy cornmeal herb triangles, fresh fruit and mini-muffins.

Photo Credits

Tea pot c. 1910, English Buffalo Pottery, Argyle pattern, provided by Jane Moody. Crystal snack sets, antique spoon, and cut glass candy and sugar bowl provided by Mary Ward.

Recipe Credits

English Breakfast Tea, recipe page 149
Belgian Waffles with Curried Chicken, recipe page 150
Cornbread Triangles with Herbs, recipe page 152

India, c. 1834 CE forward
The tea plant is found in Assam. Within a few years it has moved ahead of China in world trade.

England, c. 1840 CE forward
The Dutchess of Beford originates the custom of afternoon tea.

Tea is now produced in about 30 countries. Today India is the chief exporter, followed by China, Caucasia, Africa, Sri Lanka, Japan, Indonesia, South America, Bangladesh, Taiwan, and Malaysia.

The British Isles are still the largest importers of tea. The United States, despite its large population of coffee drinkers, ranks second. Other commonwealth countries—such as Australia, Canada, and New Zealand—also import large amounts.

In the United States a short interruption in the workday is called a coffee break. In other parts of the world, it is more likely to be a tea break. In all of Asia, Europe, the Middle East and

North Africa, tea is the more popular drink of the two. On any busy afternoon in Istanbul, Cairo, or any of several other Muslim cities, runners can be seen making their daily rounds carrying small trays of glasses filled with steaming hot tea. These are delivered to shop owners and other workers every afternoon. In many of the countries once part of the British Empire, afternoon tea is as much of a tradition as it is in Britain itself.

*S*till feeling like a novice at tea drinking, I decided to study the way the tea plant, the Camellia Sinesis, grows. I'm an avid gardener and am very aware of the difference sun, light, altitude and moisture play in the role of growing plants.

HOW TEA GROWS:

*A*ll tea originates from the evergreen Camellia Sinesis plant. As with wine and coffee, the flavor of the tea is affected by soil, tempera-ture, altitude and moisture. All tea is grown in the tropical and subtropical climates where longitude 100 degrees east crosses the Tropic of Cancer. These are jungle conditions where there is a great deal of moisture; tea, however, will not grow in a swamp. The main tea producing countries are China, India, Sri Lanka, Indonesia, Tibet, Burma, Kenya, Malawi, Tanzania, Formosa, Iran, Japan, Turkey, Bangladesh and Argentina.

Tea plants may be propagated by seedlings or by cuttings. It takes 3-5 years to grow to maturity...the seedlings grow faster at lower altitudes; high altitude teas (3000 to 7000 feet) are of superior quality. If left unattended, a tea plant would grow to a height of 30 feet. On tea gardens, or plantations, the bushes are pruned to a height of 3 feet for easy harvest.

Depending on altitude, a tea "flushes" or is ready for harvest every seven days to two weeks. When it flushes, two tiny leaves surround the seed pod. The leaves and pods are plucked. Tea pluckers, usually women, place the leaves into a basket carried on their backs or on their heads. An experienced tea plucker can harvest up to 40 pounds (19 kg) per day.

Processing

There are five stages that separate the tea drinker from the fresh leaf:

Withering

During withering, the fresh leaves are allowed to dry on trays for up to 24 hours. In this process, they lose about half their weight. They are limp and pliable.

Rolling

Done by machine or by hand, the individual leaf is rolled tip to stem, then slightly twisted to release flavor enzymes. Although the majority of tea is rolled by machine, hand rolling preserves the tip, wherein lies the greatest concentration of flavor.

Roll-Breaking

This is a machine process that breaks the tea rolls and prepares them for fermenting.

Oxidation/Fermintation

In this process...unique to black tea..the broken leaves are spread onto a glass or cement slab and allowed to oxidize and ferment for as little as one and as many as five hours. During this process, the leaves become very soft and take on a color similar to a new copper penny.

Drying/Firing

Drying can take place in wok-type cookers, in drying ovens or in drying boxes. When completed, the fermentation process is stopped and all but 3% of the moisture is removed from the leaves.

Green teas go through a similar process except that they are not fermented. Oolong teas go through several fermentation processes. Then, they are charcoal fired in baskets.

There are more than 3,000 varieties of tea. They take their names from the districts in which they grow.

After the broken grades have been sifted out, what remains are the large leaves. In brewing, flavor and color come out of leaf grades more slowly than out of broken grades. Most tea is sifted then graded by the leaf size.

These are the grades:

ORANGE PEKOE: long, thin wiry leaves. This is a size, not a quality.
PEKOE: whole leaves, but shorter and not as wiry.
SOUCHONG: a round leaf.
BROKEN ORANGE PEKOE: smaller than leaf grades and contains a bud leaf.
BROKEN PEKOE SOUCHONG: larger than broken orange pekoe.
FANNINGS: small pieces of leaf.
FINES OR DUST: the finest sift; usually used in tea bags.

Green teas and oolongs are not graded into leaf sizes.

Some teas use a different grading: green teas take into account the age and style of leaf while Japanese tea producers have a system where the name indicates the grade such as "Extra Choice" and so forth. Indian green tea and oolong have an alternate system while Formosa Oolong is graded on a one to eighteen point scale.

After the grading process, tea is sold as a commodity and shipped for export. In the United States, tea quality is regulated by the U.S. Board of Tea Experts which is under the auspices of the Food and Drug Administration. This group ensures quality and purity standards for all teas consumed in the United States.

LOOSE TEA: fine quality tea such as Orange Pekoe, Pekoe, Green tea and Oolong may be found at specialty tea shops, health food stores, in some supermarkets and in gourmet shops. Here are their names and properties:

ASSAM: this is a rich, black Indian tea.

DARJEELING: this is a special tea, grown in India's Himalayas. It has a musky flavor perfect for an afternoon energy boost or with various Indian curries. It goes well with lemon and sugar.

EARL GREY: a very popular tea, it is actually a secret blend of Bergamont Tea known only to Jackson's of Picadilly Tea Company.

ENGLISH BREAKFAST: depending on the brand, this could be a blend of any teas and generally has Assam Indian tea as well as Sri Lankan black tea. It is robust with about as much caffeine as coffee (110 mg) so it is a favorite morning tea.

FORMOSA OOLONG: a Cadillac of teas, the fruity tea is very fragrant.   A great tea to drink in between meals.

GUNPOWDER: a small green tea leaf which is curled. Very pungent, it has the least caffeine (16 mg) of teas.

JASMINE TEA: Oolong tea with Jasmine petals added. It is aromatic, flowery and light.

KEEMUM: an ancient Chinese tea grown in the Anhwei province. This tea has a superb bouquet and is known as the burgundy of teas. It can be served iced or with milk.

LAPSANG SOUCHONG: a superb tea from the Lapsang district of China. It is smoked over fires.

MAT-CHA: Japanese powdered tea leaves which are whisked into water. This tea is used in the Japanese Tea Ceremony.

NILGRI: an Indian tea grown in the southernmost tip of India. It has delicate flavor with a hint of lemon.

PU-ERH: this is a group of teas grown in the Yunnan Province of China. These teas include green, black and oolong teas and are prized for their health benefits. Earthy in flavor, they are packaged in a round brick.

RUSSIAN CARAVAN: a blend of Chinese and Oolong teas. This tea has fragrance reminiscent of a campfire.

SENCHA: a green tea that is delicious after meals.

SRI LANKAN BREAKFAST: a blend of teas from Sri Lanka. This tea has a delicate bouquet and flavor.

WHITE TEA: the most rare of all teas, this Chinese tea is not rolled or fermented...it is steamed from tea buds of the Shui Hsien White Tea plant. It makes a very delicate cup.

YUNNAN: another of the delicious teas from the Yunnan Province of China. These teas are used as a base for scented tea.

CAFFEINE:

Tea varies widely in the amount of caffeine per cup. A cup of green tea may have nearly no caffeine while a cup of Assam that has been infused (brewed) for five minutes may have up to 120 milligrams (mg) of caffeine, almost equal to that of coffee. The reason? In general, the longer the tea leaves have fermented, the greater the concentration of caffeine. The shorter the infusion (or brewing) time, the less the caffeine. As tea leaves become smaller and more broken (fannings, fines and dust), the concentrations of caffeine become greater.

WHY THE CONCERN?

Caffeine is a mild stimulant that increases urination and speeds up heart rate and rhythm. After drinking a couple of cups of Assam tea, one might feel an increase in the association of ideas, a sense of euphoria or an increased ability to learn and memorize numbers, concepts and thought sequences. We can attribute these to caffeine. However, the effect is not without limits: the body can absorb only 300 mg of caffeine during an 8-hour period, so going beyond that (the fifth and sixth cups of caffeinated tea) actually has little additional impact. Caffeine's primary effect lasts only about 45 minutes.

Caffeine contributes to the flavors of tea. But for some individuals, caffeine in tea may cause "jitters." For this reason, a chart has been created on page 21. This indicates, approximately, the amount of caffeine in different teas. Most medical authorities find three hundred milligrams (mg) of caffeine to be a "safe" level.

The quantity of any given tea will be reduced by shortening the infusion process. Black tea infused for 3 minutes has 50 mg of caffeine whereas the same tea infused for 5 minutes has 100 mg. Tea bags may be rich in caffeine as their tea dust releases caffeine into the hot beverage very quickly.

Leading health organizations have studied the effects of caffeine on health. Their findings indicate that caffeinated tea, when consumed in moderation, does not pose a threat to health. However, if the reader has a history of heart arrhythmia, stomach ulcers, fibrocystic disease or if pregnant, drink a green or oolong tea or a tea which has been infused for a short period of time.

DECAFFEINATED TEA:

Tea is decaffeinated at the very end of its processing...after withering, rolling, roll-breaking, drying, fermenting and firing. The process removes all but about 4% of the caffeine and most of the flavor. Most decaffeinated teas have added natural and artificial scents and flavors to the tea.

If the reader is caffeine sensitive and does not enjoy decaffeinated tea, it's a marvelous idea is to create a tea blend from a green or oolong tea which has been blended with herbs. Chapter 3 has many wonderful herbal teas.

How Much Caffeine In A 6 Ounce (185 ml) Cup of Tea?

TEA DESCRIPTION	MILLIGRAMS
Black Tea, loose or bag, infused 5 minutes	120
Black Tea, loose or bag, infused 3 minutes	46
Canned Iced Tea	36
Black Tea, loose or bag, infused 1 minute	33
Instant Tea	28
Oolong Tea, infused maximum 15 minutes	55
Green Tea, infused maximum 15 minutes	16
Decaffeinated tea	4

Sources: Dawn Campbell/Nancy Friedman

After finishing my research, I decided that to do a "proper" book on tea, I'd need two elements: a teaist (or tea artist) and an excellent creative design team. Why the backup when I've written more than 10 cookbooks? Because it takes more than recipes to do a great book. It takes great design, great beauty and great knowledge.

So, I went to my longtime, dear friends, Donna Morris (an award-winning graphic artist) and to Barney Taxel (an award-winning photographic illustrator). Both were enthusiastic about the tea book project. Donna designed all graphics for this book as well as layout for the photography and on-camera styling. Barney carefully executed these layouts onto film. As you look through this book, remember the long, but loving, hours spent on all the design and photographic elements of this book. Remember also the fun and pleasure of kitchen testing and sharing tastings of these recipes with my friends...young and old.

Next, Donna directed me to Daniel Mantey, proprietor of "The Wabi Shop", a tea shop in the Murray Hill district of Cleveland, Ohio. Daniel, also a tea artist, not only provided us with many of the props used in photography, he has acted as a mentor in my own discoveries on the joys of tea drinking. Daniel guided Donna, Barney, Barney's wife Laura (a writer herself), and myself through his lovely adaptation of The Japanese Tea Ceremony. Daniel and I have also spent much time in collaboration for the first two chapters of this book. When it comes to tea, Daniel has tremendous knowledge. He uses tea as his artistic medium, coaxing unbelievable flavors from his endless varieties of teas. His frequent buying trips to the Orient ensure current knowledge and the best product. He's a tea picker, a tea master, a teaist, a perfectionist and a purist. He presents his thoughts on making the perfect cup of tea in the next chapter.

Life is beautiful. Drink tea and see.

Chinese Tea

The Chinese actually prepare tea in tiny teapots and drink this delicious tea in tiny cups. Nuts would be a fine accompaniment. In our Chinese ceremony, western tea pot and cup are actually used while traditional Chinese tea pot and cups are the focus of admiration.

Photo Credits
Chinese Turn-of-the-Century Made for Western Market Tea Pot. Chinese 1930's Tea Cup. Jade Lion, c. 1850 CE. Chinese Tea Set with Cups: Gong-Fu. Water Ewer from the T'ang Dynasty, c. 300 CE.Brown Tea Pot: prototype of Ming Dynasty Tea Pot. All Chinese tea products provided by Daniel Mantey, The Wabi Shop, Cleveland, Ohio 44106.

Recipe Credit
International Tea Ceremonies and Traditions, pages 135-165

2 THE PERFECT CUP OF TEA

BY DANIEL MANTEY

The perfect cup of tea? Mary asked me at one of our sessions, "So how do you make a perfect cup of tea?" To which I asked, "Which tea?" I could have also asked, "Who's tea...yours or mine?"

And thats just for starts. There is no single way to make any perfect cup, or pot, or bowl of tea. It all depends on the which, what, why, who, when, and where of the tea at hand. Making tea, is first a science, and then an art. But it's a science you can learn rather quickly as you go along, and an art that will surprise, relax, and satisfy you beyond your expectations.

BEGIN AT THE BEGINNING:

Let's start with some basics. I will always refer to tea from the Camillia Sinesis plant, not herbal tea tisanes, though the same techniques could apply to both. Tea, by the time you get it, is a dried, somewhat shriveled, leaf or bits and pieces of leaf. As a leaf, it has plant cell-structures that, though broken, or rolled, or smashed, are still intact. What we want to do, by adding hot water,

is to get these little plant cells to open up and
release all their wonderful oils, juices, and flavors
into the water we are about to drink. That sounds
easy enough, and once we begin to understand
the nature of these tea leaves, we will be making
great tea.

As a tea-artist (aren't you excited already?), you must first study the tea you are about
to prepare. We will get to tea-bags (yes, I use,
and quite enjoy bagged tea), but I must point out
that any serious tea drinker, when speaking of
"tea," is referring to a beverage made from loose
leaves. For now, any loose tea will do. If you
don't have some loose tea, read on, and make
sure you get some your next time out.

Pour some tea leaves onto a small plate.
Are they still recognizable as leaves? Teas will vary
a lot depending on how the tea was processed.
An Oolong's leaves are rolled, and smashed over a
dozen times before firing, and look like tiny writh-
ing dark dragons (guess what Oolong means).
Gun-Powder tea leaves are rolled until they look
like tiny little pellets of, yes, you guessed it.

Dragon-Well Tea (named after the Well where the tea first grew, and the well water which was originally used) is flat, and shiny from being hand-pressed against a hot wok. Japanese green teas look like tiny slivers of emerald grass. Indian, and African teas, vary from large, almost whole leaves to all sizes of broken leaves, down to tiny bits and pieces. These are referred to as Orthodox teas. Many of these teas are now prepared using a CTC method (cut-tear-chop by machine, refered to as unorthodox teas) producing a tea which, to the eye, nearly resembles ground coffee. For simplicity, in the rest of this chapter, I will refer to Indian and African teas collectively as "English" tea, as it is the English market which has created this style of tea and leaf. The rule of thumb: the more intact the leaf, the slower it will release its nectar; the smaller the leaf particles, the quicker your work is done.

GLORIOUS COLORS:

Is your tea black, red, green, or white? When you purchased your tea, you were told which of the above it is. Most "English" teas are black. Chinese teas are white, green, or red (they name the color after the beverage, not the leaf), or somewhere in between. Most Japanese teas are green. (All tea, of course, starts out as a green leaf; we won't get into that now.) The color of the leaf on your plate may not correspond exactly to the color designated, but don't worry. First, you need to know which it is, and then which color it looks like. The whiter and greener the tea, the more delicate the leaf is, the more tender the cell structure. The darker the tea, the more hardy and fool-proof the leaf. The color name, and the visual color will eventually give you the subtle clues as to how to treat the leaf.

MAGIC IN THE WATER:

The water. Tea is mostly water, after all. There are so many wonderful "tea-water" stories from long ago: imagine making your tea with water that came from the melted snow, from the branches of a plum-tree in bloom on the Yellow Mountain! But I'll save those stories for your own discovery. We need to be more practical, so I will recommend filtered and spring water;

but some city water can have a nice taste. I rather enjoyed the tap-water of Oberlin, Ohio, when I was doing my Masters Degree there. This past fall, a Taiwanese tea-friend told me she uses a cup of tap water to every quart of spring water, to insure an interesting character!

There are songs about the water of Boston, and Dubliners love their water I'm told. The chlorine is the culprit in most cases, and perhaps that is boiled out as the kettle warms up. But don't use already boiled water if you can help it. It has a very flat taste. I've read so many reasons why; I don't know which is true: No oxygen? Maybe no chlorine?

TO BUBBLE OR NOT:

Water Temperature. I no longer use boiling water! The whiter and greener the leaf, generally the cooler the water; the blacker or redder, the hotter. When I think of leaves in hot water, I think of myself taking a nice, hot bath. I like it hot, but not too hot. We want our little leaves to stretch out and unfurl; we want those little cells to moisten and expand. We want to coax those little leaves to give us an unforgettable little brew. We don't want to scald or cook the tea! We don't want to cause a chemical reaction to occur. We want what's in those leaves to get into the water for us to drink. That's all.

POTS n' BAGS

You will eventually need a tea-pot. I know, you use a mug. You probably also use a microwave to "heat" the water (more like "zap it"). And eventually, face it, tea is "in", you will need lots of tea-pots in lots of different sizes and types, and colors. Maybe even two of each size (I will explain the two-pot method soon). But we will start things off easy for you, to put some of the science into practice.

In fact, we will start with a tea-bag, and a mug!

Tea bags really aren't that bad after all. But it does depend on who made the tea-bag. I love Lipton's Yellow-label tea bags! Red Rose,

Jackson's, Williamson & Magor; most of your reputable loose-tea companies make reputable tea-bags—in order to stay in business. Tea-bags are quick, easy, and neat: all three are very important at the work-place, in offices, dorms, when camping or places where a sink is not at hand. Remember... tea-bags are to tea, what hamburgers are to filet mignon! But tea-bags will get us started.

PERFECTION FROM A TEA BAG:

Get your mug, your tea-bag, a teaspoon, and a small plate. I will hope you have a kettle as well. No, do not use your Mr. Coffee to heat the water, please!. We haven't made our full list of tea utensils yet, but you must also get a timer. Not one of those silent sand-filled egg-timers, but a timer with a nice noticeable ring.

I like those electric kettles that are showing up at some stores. The English have had them for some time now, with automatic shut-off, and flashing lights, and all sorts of safety features.

But let's start the kettle warming. Have you ever really listened to a kettle warm up to a boil? As soon as the kettle starts to "knock," pour some water into the mug to heat it up, and put the small plate on top of it. Now listen. We want to create the stage that the Japanese refer to as "wind blowing through the pine trees." It is that soft roar just before the quieter roll of the full boil. If you can catch it, great, if not, turn off the kettle when it hits the boil, and let it sit.

At this point, empty out the mug, drop in the tea bag, and cover it again with the plate. Give the water in the kettle about 20 seconds to sit. Then, pour the water into the mug and over the tea-bag, put the plate over the cup, and wait. Never put a tea bag into the water; it's too late. Shame on all those restaurants that bring you luke warm water in a pot or mug, and a tea bag on a plate!

Set the time for two minutes and wait. When the bell rings, remove the plate, pull out the tea-bag, set the bag in the spoon, wrap the string around the bag until the label sits on top of it, squeeze the bag into the mug, and set the spoon and spent bag onto the plate.

A lot more has just happened than you probably think. You can now drink your tea. And just for the experiment, try the tea without any additives...try several sips, in fact. Wait a minute and sip some more. We are developing technique now, so we won't add anything yet, but later on, we will discuss additives.

TIMING IS EVERYTHING:

Most tea-bags, and certainly the good ones, use CTC tea leaves. Tea companies cannot afford to put expensive large leaves in a tea-bag, which means the tea will steep quickly. Some experts claim that tea-bag tea is fully steeped in thirty seconds. You've just tasted a two minute tea; now, each time you make your tea, vary the steeping length from thirty seconds up to two minutes, and then from two minutes up to five. Try getting a little journal and write down your reactions.

For the most part, brewing for five minutes is the max. In my book, three and a half minutes is the max. The rule of thumb: up to two minutes, a fragrant tea; up to four minutes, less fragrance, but more taste; after five minute, bitter! This is because of the tannic acids, or tannins that we want to avoid. We want to avoid them not only for a better, less bitter taste, but also because some experts claim once they are in the blood stream, they prevent the absorption of iron. Green teas have no tannins.

Back to our tea. How big is your mug? The ratio of water to tea-bag is, of course, important, but I'll let you figure that out. Adding hot water to already steeped tea weakens the taste, but it doesn't change it. Remember that!

PREPARE FOR LOOSE TEA BREWING:

We are now ready for the big time... here's your list of tea utensils:

- a tea-pot
- a second tea pot of the same or larger size, or a ceramic or porcelain pitcher

- a teaspoon (now you know why it's called a "tea" spoon)
- a small plate (to hold the measured tea leaves)
- a tea strainer (any small kitchen strainer will do)
- a kettle (no microwaves allowed from here on in)
- a tea cup (mugs are not used for drinking tea!)
- water (see section on page 30)
- tea (loose, at this point an "English" tea is best)
- a timer (do not rely on just watching the clock!)
- a hot pad
- a mug (this mug is for the "waste water")
- optional: a cozy, or a candle-tea-warmer

Notice, I did not include a "tea-ball-infuser!" I think those should be made illegal. The tea-pot is already your infuser! The leaves need to float about and react in the water. So much flavor is lost, locked in those despicable "tea-prisons." And yes, I know many of you use French coffee presses. They actually do work quite well, but they do take some of the romance out of tea making, and you shouldn't use the same one

*that you make your coffee in. In Japan and Tai-
wan, these are sold and used only as "tea-pots!"
Tea-pots are so cool; do get some.*

*What we did on the previous pages with
the mug and tea-bag, created most of the correct
conditions of a tea-pot and loose tea. The plate-
covered mug was our make-shift tea-pot. An open
mug loses too much heat to the air.*

*How big is your tea-pot? And how
much tea do you want to make? Always make as
much tea as you are basically going to drink immediately. The ratio of tea-leaves to cups of tea is
important, but is a ratio that depends on the type
of tea and the strength you desire. The idea of
"one for each cup and one for the pot" was invented by some tea company that wanted the
consumer to buy more tea.*

*I generally use one teaspoon of tea
leaves for every two cups that I will drink. Now
do realize, a tea cup is only four ounces! No*

mugs allowed! With darjeelings and Tippy Assams I use even less tea. If it's my breakfast tea, I might go a bit more than a teaspoon per two cups. Experiment, and take note. We will discuss some good ways to experiment with our teas in the following pages.

Now with our tea-pot and loose tea, let's go through the whole steeping process again. I'll assume you have a clean tea-pot, but if not, now is the time to clean it. Cleaning tea things usually means only rinsing them with very hot (even boiling) water, using mild dish-soap and a soft sponge only when needed to clean the outside. I never clean the inside of a tea-pot. Unlike coffee, tea-leaves do not leave (no pun intended) an oily, acidy residue. Tea does leave a dark brown stain, but many tea lovers cherish that stain. Our tea-cups at home are all dark brown inside. The Chinese are almost fanatical about never cleaning tea-pots or cups, and those beautiful unglazed Yi-xing tea pots are the main reason why. They "say" that eventually, with a seasoned tea-pot, you don't even need to add tea.

BREW THE HEAVENLY ELIXIR:

Fill the kettle and start the burner.
While the kettle is warming up, line up all your
utensils. Measure out your leaves and put them
on the small plate. Admire the weather outside,
practice deep breathing, read some of the old
"Calvin and Hobbes" cartoons clipped to your
fridge...but don't watch the kettle.

When the kettle starts to "knock," pour
some hot water into the first pot, put its lid back
on and put the kettle back on the stove. As the
boil approaches, get ready for some quick action.
Pour the hot water from the first pot into the
second pot (or pitcher), pour the measured tea
leaves into the first pot (to steam them up a bit),
put the lid back on both pots, turn off the kettle,
count to about twenty.

At twenty, fill the first pot with the just
boiled water, making sure the leaves get a good
churning in the process. Put the lid back on, set
the timer for two minutes, pour the water out of
the second pot and into the mug. Pour some

Japanese Tea

Reflection, respect, reverence...a Japanese tea ceremony is like none other. A delicious green tea accompanies the moment. For Japanese style tea, somber color combined with authenticity are key.

Photo Credits
Shigaraki green tea ensemble, modern. Lacquer tray: modern Japanese. Other equipage: kettle, brazier, water scoop and ash rake: late Edo period. Shinobue bamboo flute. All Japanese tea products provided by Daniel Mantey, The Wabi Shop, Cleveland, Ohio 44106.

Recipe Credit
Green Tea (Mat-Cha) described in Chapter 2 (page 50) and on page 146

boiled water from the kettle into pot number two and into your tea cup.

Get the strainer ready, watch the timer. Empty out the second pot...ding! Now, open the first pot and with your teaspoon give the tea one good swirl, replace the lid, put the strainer over the opened second pot and pour the contents of the first pot into the second pot

When pouring tea, always keep your second hand on the tea-pot's lid—always. There are too many broken lids and cups already! Empty the tea cup into the mug, carry the now filled second pot and your warmed tea cup to the table and sit down.

Pour yourself a cup of tea.

If we didn't use the second pot (or pitcher), the leaves would still be in the tea, getting too strong and too bitter. A tea cozy over the pot will help it stay warm, or a tea warmer with a "tea-candle" under the pot, will keep it very hot

(as the Northern Europeans do). The pitcher is fine
for the summer when the weather, and the tea
needn't stay so hot.

Enjoy your tea.

Allow me to say a few more words
about cleaning tea things. After you've finished
your tea is the best time to clean up everything.
Rinse out both pots, pour any used leaves in a sink
strainer, and put the leaves in the garden or some
flower pots for mulch. Use the "waste-water" in
the mug to water the nearest plant. Your kettle
will still be hot so give everything a last rinse with
hot water. You will be ready the next time you
want some tea. Every once in a while, you might
shine up the outside of your cups and pots, but—
other than that—you don't need to do any major
scrubbing ever. This is quite different from coffee
clean-up procedures! Scrubbing cups and pots may
ruin their decoration. And do be so careful at the
sink. Most tea-pots are broken against kitchen
faucets...especially spouts.

REFLECTIONS:

Now, what we just went through is quite a bit of very serious tea-making technique. It would be good to read through it several times. Then put it to daily practice. But we are in no hurry. I love tea, but I only drink it two or three times a day. The tea-bag experiments alone represent a good few weeks of tea drinking. Of course, you can substitute tea-bags for the loose tea in the second procedure and follow pretty much the same pattern.

This technique will work for nearly every tea you come across, though it is specifically for "English" tea. (I will discuss Chinese and Japanese later.) It is your preference to decide: 1) how much loose tea, 2) how long to wait for the water to cool (unless you are getting into especially green teas, 30 seconds should do), 3) how long to steep, and the additives. We're almost there.

Plan a regimen for comparing all your teas. For instance, line up all your loose tea tins (we have 21 on the kitchen shelf), and use a

different tea each day. Decide upon the parameters for each tea session: one teaspoon of leaves
to every two cups, thirty second kettle cool down,
two minutes steep (for loose tea, two minutes is
the minimum steeping time), and use the same
conditions for each tea. Take notes, change the
parameters for the next session and compare.

Some teas will seem strong, others
weak, and some just right. This could take
months, but what an adventure and there is no
other way to do it. You may also use one tea for a
whole week, and change the parameters daily to
compare the resulting beverages. That way, you
can really zero in on your preference for each tea's
aroma, color and taste. Your tea journal is getting
quite full and interesting by now.

So you see you need to decide what is
a perfect cup of tea, and then you need to know
how to achieve it. You are the one drinking it,
and it has to satisfy your tastes and needs.

Speaking of needs, that's a whole other
question. Are you making the tea for: the

caffeine; a hot something to drink; something to go with a meal; an afternoon break or perhaps just to enjoy the taste of a special tea? It's your choice.

Tea pots. If you're not used to them, then just go out and buy one or two and see how they work. Buy some just for looks, buy small ones, big ones, old ones, new ones. If they don't work well, put them on the shelf for decoration or give them away as house warming gifts. The same with tea cups. And once you've gotten a feel for pots and cups, get a nice full set. My wife and I have so much fun enjoying our breakfast tea every morning with our delicate 1920's Czechoslovakian tea set. Some tea pots have built in infusers. Those are sort of all right...but why not be brave...just let the leaves float about on their own, and use the tea strainer over the cup, or second pot. And it's really all right if some leaves do get into your cup. Tea leaves are not coffee grounds. Besides, if there are no tea leaves in your cup, how can you ever read your tea leaves?

MILK AND HONEY:

 Additives. There is nothing wrong with adding milk to tea, or sweetening it. Again, you're drinking the tea, but here are my suggestions. I use honey to sweeten tea, and just a tiny dab. And I use regular milk...just a splash. Sugar is simply too sweet and cream adds too much flavor. Skim milk is too wimpy, artificial sweeteners and powdered creamers taste so awful that I hope you don't need to use either. Lemon is for iced tea.

 Experiment. Perhaps, as I've suggested earlier, you now have already tried all of your teas under many different steeping conditions without any additives, and perhaps you've decided you now like them that way! But do some experiments with honey only, or milk only, and see what happens. I love Lapsang Souchong with milk but without honey. Breakfast blends, which I usually make extra strong, I love with lots of both. Darjeelings and Russian teas, not to be confused with Russian Caravan, I usually leave alone. Speaking of Russian teas, here's a fun Russianesque idea. Every time you get to the end of a jar of jam or preserves, "clean" it out with your just steeped tea. Put a spoon in the jar first, so that the glass doesn't crack, and swoosh it all around. Add milk; see what you think. And, please, always taste a tea before adding anything — especially when you are a guest sampling $300 a pound First Flush Prize Darjeeling!

HISTORICALLY SPEAKING:

When we think of tea, we usually think of the English, and that, after all, is because the English gave us our tea during the Colonial days, and we promptly dumped it all in the harbor.

The rest of Northern Europe has a lot to offer as far as tea technique. In fact, my brewing technique might owe more to the French and Flemish than to the English. The Dutch also have a wonderful feel for tea! However, the English and the rest of Europe are historically relatively "new kids" on the "tea block." We are the newest, and India fits in between (you will be so surprised as you read up on your tea history). European customs of tea making only go back to about 1650. On the other hand, the Chinese have been drink-

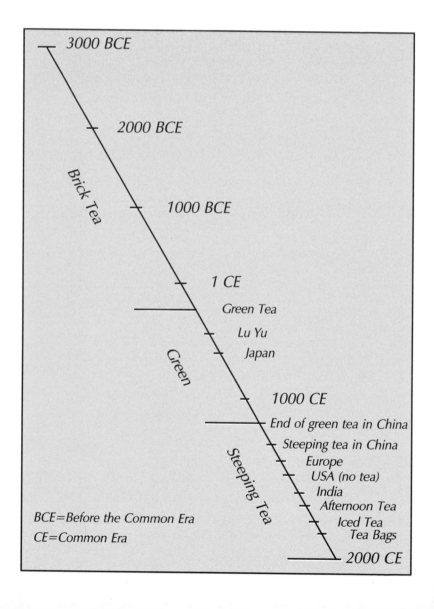

3000 BCE

2000 BCE

Brick Tea

1000 BCE

1 CE

Green Tea

Lu Yu

Japan

Green

1000 CE

End of green tea in China

Steeping tea in China

Europe

USA (no tea)

India

Steeping Tea

Afternoon Tea

Iced Tea

Tea Bags

BCE=Before the Common Era

CE=Common Era

2000 CE

ing tea for nearly 5000 years, and the Japanese for well over 1000 years. Africa is now producing absolutely beautiful tea.

Mary wrote a time line in Chapter 1, and on the preceeding page is a visual time line to help put things into perspective.

ANCIENT TIMES IN CHINA & JAPAN:

So now we turn to China and Japan. There are three distinct episodes of Chinese tea history: Brick Tea, Green Tea and Steeped Tea.

Brick tea was the very earliest method of processing tea in China. It is made by steaming the tea leaves and then pressing them into a brick mold. A chunk of the brick was broken off and tossed into a big pot of boiling water, and cooked like a stew with additional ingredients. The oldest tea recipes call for onions, garlic, and salt. Tea was originally more of a soup than a beverage. The Tibetan style of tea to this day still uses a similar recipe. Pu-erh and Tribute tea from China are still made and sold by the brick. As time passed, the soup evolved into a sweet mixture rather than salty, with sugar, spices, and fruits mixed into the brew. The North Indian Chai is the modern day descendent of this recipe. Bricks were actually minted and used as money, for buying horses or whatever.

Green tea. Around the turn of the Millennium, tea was produced in quite a different way. The freshly picked green tea leaves were steamed, to kill the enzymes (hence, no oxidation), dried and pulverized. A vivid chartreuse green powder resulted. This tea was whipped in a bowl of hot water and drunk. An elaborate ritualistic ceremony eventually evolved, especially in the Chan Buddhist Monasteries of China, and this became the way to drink tea for the next 1000 years!

Around 1400 CE, the method of steeping tea came into fashion, and eventually the tea pot was invented. It was soon after that trade with the West began, and soon the whole world was drinking tea steeped in tea pots. The tea pot, though, was not an entirely new invention...it evolved from the wine and water ewers that had been around in China for centuries. In the photo of the Chinese Tea Service, a T'ang-dynasty water ewer sits in the back left. (The lid is about 1000 years older than the ewer.)

The Chinese invented a very special way of steeping tea, using tiny fist-sized tea-pots, and tiny cups that held barely an ounce of tea at a time. This is the way that one should steep a good Chinese tea. This method in mainland China is referred to as "Gong-fu-cha," meaning "hard-work-tea," and in Taiwan, where it is the absolute rage as I write this, it is called "Lau-ren-cha," meaning "old-men's-tea." Before this style became fashionable ten years ago, it was only practiced by old men, and usually at night, out of doors on the quiet city back streets. The very delicate tea set in the foreground of the Chinese photo is a mainland set for this style of tea. This way of steeping and drinking tea brings out the very unique characteristics of Chinese teas, especially those of the high mountain Oolongs of Taiwan. This technique is very difficult to master and requires much time, the right tools, and the right tea. This is the house specialty of my teahouse "The Wabi Shop" up in Cleveland, Ohio. In time, this kind of ceremony might make itself known all over America, as the Yi-xing tea pots are making such a hit over here.

This is a recipe book after all, and this chapter is already perhaps too weighty, so I will only say, that concerning Chinese Tea, there is an entire new universe out there for you to explore (once you've got your "English" teas down).

And Japanese teas! This, too, is beyond the scope of this chapter and book. The Japanese still drink the powdered Ma-cha, and actually I will say a few words about that. Read up on the Japanese Tea Ceremony, or go to Japan and learn about it, or visit "The Wabi Shop" and experience a Japanese Tea Ceremony.   Ceremony aside, Ma-cha is a very easy tea to make, and very healthy (many Western doctors report on its benefits!). It also has a great caffeine rush! Once you get some Ma-cha (it is available ...see Mail Order at the end of this book), all you need is a neat bowl, a small whisk (a tiny egg whisk is OK but don't scratch the bowl) and some hot water. And I mean hot — not boiling... Stop the kettle after the first knock (remember, "knock" from the beginning of this chapter). Put a scant 1/4 teaspoon of Ma-cha in your bowl, add about 1/4 cup of water, whisk 'til frothy, and drink. Mary could have included a green tea ice cream recipe in this, but I'll save her the trouble: mix Ma-cha with vanilla ice cream and eat!

The Japanese also have a marvelous ritual of drinking their green leaf tea (sencha) which is very similar to the Chinese gong-fu style, and a tea set for that is pictured in the Japanese Tea photo. (I confess, the black tea caddie is for Ma-cha, not Sen-cha, but it looked so good in the photo).

Both the Chinese and Japanese methods of preparing tea are very time consuming, and beautifully so, and require so much attention that really these teas are difficult to do in the context of cooking and eating. In both countries, these styles of tea drinking are not done with a meal, but sometimes after a meal. For the recipes of this book, use the "English" style I have taught earlier with your Chinese and Japanese tea, and remember to keep the water far from boiling, the greener the tea.

I'm just about out of here. I cannot believe I've actually gotten through this much tea information. But a few closing remarks before you get on with the incredible recipes ahead.

America is waking up to tea. Soon there might just be Tea Shops on every other corner (tea and coffee really can't mix in the same store, so be wary of the coffee shops that start pushing tea; tea absorbs odors so easily that tea leaves in a coffee shop will taste like coffee!!!) Already, many teas from all over the world are available in some very fine shops. More will open. Welcome to this adventure. And, there is a tea magazine out there, in its third year: Tea, A Magazine. It is available through P.O. Box 348, Scotland, CT 06264.

The November/December, 1995, issue had a wonderful article on the Chinese Tea Ritual I mentioned earlier, and you can begin to connect with the serious tea drinkers of the world through all of the information in the magazine. Read as many of the books in the bibliography as you can get. I know two of my favorites are already out of print: A Time for Tea by Jason Goodwin and The Chinese Art of Tea by John Blofield. John has those lovely stories about tea water mentioned earlier in this chapter. Try to find them! But James Norwood Pratt's, A Tea Lover's Treasury has just been reprinted (though they didn't review his opinions of Pu-ehr tea, or the Japanese Tea Ceremony!). This treasury is easily the most comprehensive book on tea on the market, in my opinion the best, and a joy to read.

One last word: iced tea. I love iced tea. Considering we have drunk it for nearly a century, iced tea is the only tea known to many Americans... and what a business it now is! The rest of the world has only begun to drink it in the last 5 to 10 years. Taiwan began in 1987. I know; I was there. Northern Europe didn't in 1985, but it does now. I'm not sure exactly when they started. Most of that bottled stuff out there is absolutely horrible. As far as I'm concerned, there is only one way to make iced tea...use the earlier methods to make your perfect pot of hot tea, and make a huge pot of it. Let it cool down, put it in the fridge overnight. The next day, you will have iced tea...perfect iced tea! I've always enjoyed the slow and simple things in life, and tea is one of them.

Happy steeping, and happy drinking.

Daniel Mantey

Grandma's Kitchen Tea

...whether you are a grandmother or a grandmother wannabe, the ingredients for this fun tea include imagination and simplicity. Start with a yummy hot tea recipe...add a few scones and a lot of love. Use the most whimsical tea pot with the most fun kitchenware imaginable.

Photo Credits

Tomato tea set provided by Affordable Antiques, Lakewood, Ohio 44107. Antique jelly jars and Greek plate provided by Mary Ward. Whimsical carrot top salt and pepper shakers provided by Donna Morris.

Recipe Credits

Autumn Apple Tea, recipe page 62
Iced Cherry Scones, recipe page 157

3 HOT TEAS:
HOT TEAS, HERB BLENDS, MEDICINAL TEAS & INFUSIONS

ABOUT THE RECIPES:

Nutritional values for the recipes in this book have been computed using Nutritionist III®, version 7.2, First Data Bank (formerly N-Squared Computing), San Bruno, California. Nutritional values for all recipes include calories, % calories from fat, total fat, saturated fat, cholesterol, sodium and caffeine. In addition, all recipes include international metric measurements for weight, liquid and temperature. Ingredients for most recipes may be found in tea shops, health food stores, in gourmet shops and in many large supermarkets. If the ingredients are not readily available in the reader's market, use the mail order sources, listed in the back of this book.

HOT TEAS:
HEALTH BENEFITS OF HOT TEA

First and foremost, hot teas are healthful because they are hot. When hot water is used to make a beverage, it has a soothing quality. In addition, the vapors from the heat act to relax and refresh nasal and breathing passages. Additionally, if water is impure, heating it will kill any lingering bacteria and/or germs. Increasingly, the health benefits of tea are being studied. The following are some of the better known health attributes of tea:

- the essential oils and polyphenols are an aid to digestion.
- tea contains 1.32 - 4.18 ppm of fluoride. That's twice the quantity of flouride in fluoridated water.
- tea is low in calories; 4 calories per 6 ounce cup.
- green teas are thought to be a preventive to lung cancer, antioxidants and a beverage with a considerable amount of vitamin C.
- teas, in general, are soothing to bug bites, and are known to dry them out. Tea bags are a refresher to tired eyes.

HOT TEAS FROM AROUND THE WORLD

To make the finest tea, loose tea leaves have been used in all recipes. Loose tea is available at tea shops, in health food stores, in gourmet stores and in some supermarkets. As the reader will note, after reading Daniel Mantey's fine tea commentary in Chapter 2, infusing tea is an art form...using temperature, time and talent, tea can evolve and emerge into different flavors and strengths. For the purposes of tea celebrations, the author has taken the liberty to use tea as an ingredient in most of these recipes. Generally, the author recommends about 1 teaspoon of tea per serving. Blended with the other ingredients, that is an amount of tea pleasing to many palates. However, more or less tea may be used. Generally, the darker the tea leaf, the bolder the flavor.

AUTUMN APPLE TEA

6 ounces
(185 ml) water

1 teaspoon
(5 gm) tea green
or black tea
leaves

1 teaspoon
(5gm) honey

1 apple, peeled
and chopped
into small pieces

*...a refreshing way to make tea —
especially in the fall when apples are at
their peak. This recipe originated in the
Ukraine.*

Serves: 1

Brew the tea according to directions in
Chapter 2. Place apple into a small
bowl. After steeping, pour tea over the
apple. To serve: eat apple pieces with a
spoon and drink the tea from the bowl.

Each serving: 104 calories; 4% calories from fat; less
than 1 gm total fat; 00 gm saturated fat; 00 mg
cholesterol; 6 mg sodium; 35 mg caffeine.

BILLY BREW

Here's the famous tea referenced in "Waltzing Matilda" ("...and he sang as he watched and waited 'til his Billy brews, you'll come a waltzing Matilda with me.") This is a strong tea the Australians make in a "Billy" or a large can.

Serves: 6

4 cups(1 liter) water

4 teaspoons (20 gm) black tea
1 tablespoon (15 gm) honey

Heat water to a boil. Add tea and continue to boil for 15 minutes. Just before serving, add honey to the brew. Strain tea or drink with leaves.

Each serving: 19 calories; 00% calories from fat; 00 gm total fat; 00 gm saturated fat; 00 mg cholesterol; 8 mg sodium; 50 mg caffeine.

CEYLON SPICED TEA

1 teaspoon
(5 gm) carda-
mom seeds or
powder

1 cinnamon stick

3 slices fresh
ginger root

2 teaspoons
(10 gm) orange
zest

4 teaspoons
(20 gm) Ceylon
tea leaves

3 cups (750 ml)
water

Traditionally, Sri Lankans have rules for making tea: use high quality tea leaves, freshly drawn water, rinse the teapot to warm, bring the water to a rolling boil, bring the teapot to the boiling water for maximum heat, allow the tea to steep for 5 minutes, and stir the pot of tea before serving.

Serves: 4

Place cardamom seeds, cinnamon, ginger, orange zest and tea leaves into a teapot. In a separate pot, heat the water to a fast boil, bring the teapot to the stove and pour water into tea pot. Steep for 5 minutes, stir the tea and strain into cups.

Each serving: 5 calories; 00% calories from fat; 00 gm total fat; 00 gm saturated fat; 00 mg cholesterol; 6 mg sodium; 36 mg caffeine.

CHINA TEA CAKE TEA

This method of infusing tea has been used for centures in China. It is a very syrupy tea. Flavored rice cakes may be used as well.

Serves: 4

In a small saucepan, blend rice cakes, tea, ginger and water. Bring to a boil and stir to cook and dissolve rice cakes. When mixture is thick and syrupy, strain into cups. Drink immediately.

Each serving: 37 calories; 1% calories from fat; less than 1 gm total fat; 00 gm saturated fat; 00 mg cholesterol; 7 mg sodium; 47 mg caffeine.

4 regular sized rice cakes (120 gm)

4 teaspoons (20 gm) green tea leaves

2 slices fresh ginger

3 cups (750 ml) water

CHRISTMAS SLEMP TEA

3 cups (750 ml) milk

2 cinnamon sticks

2 teaspoons (10 gm) whole cloves

1 teaspoon (5 gm) aniseed

2 thin strips orange peel

2 thin strips lemon peel

2 teaspoons (10 gm) green tea leaves

1 large piece of cheesecloth

2 tablespoons (30 gm) corn-starch

2 tablespoons (30 ml) water

1/3 cup (85 gm) sugar

Here's a delicious milk tea that is sure to please children and grown ups alike.

Serves: 4

In a large pot, heat milk until it is a near-boil. Meanwhile, tie cinnamon, cloves, aniseed, orange peel, lemon peel and tea leaves into the cheesecloth square allowing for 100% expansion room. When milk is hot, place cheese-cloth bag in pot, cover and remove from heat. Allow to steep for 5 minutes. Remove cheesecloth bag. In a small bowl, blend cornstarch and water into a smooth paste. Whisk into the hot milk mixture along with sugar. Heat milk and whisk until mixture is thick, about 5 minutes. Serve in warmed mugs.

Each serving: 151 calories; 4% calories from fat; 7 gm total fat; less than 1 gm saturated fat; 3 mg cholesterol; 102 mg sodium; 24 mg caffeine.

CRANBERRY TEA

Keep a few cranberries in the freezer year round for this tasty brew.

Serves: 4

Place fresh or frozen and defrosted cranberries into a teapot with tea and honey. In a separate pot, heat water to a near-boil. Pour into tea pot. Allow to steep for 5 minutes. To serve, strain into tea cups and garnish with apple slices.

Each serving: 41 calories; less than 1% calories from fat; less than 1 gm total fat; 00 gm saturated fat; 00 mg cholesterol; 7 mg sodium; 47 mg caffeine.

1/2 cup (120 gm) cranberries, fresh or frozen

4 teaspoons (20 gm) black tea leaves

4 teaspoons (20 gm) honey

3 cups (750 ml) water

4 thin slices of apple

FORMOSA SOUR SCENTED TEA

1 large orange

1/2 cup
(120 gm) black
tea leaves

It's fun to make this tea...and it has a wonderful, smoky flavor. Traditionally, it was served in Formosa (now Taiwan) tea houses. Once prepared, the tea leaves can be refrigerated and used for 2 weeks.

Serves: 24

With a sharp knife, cut the top off the orange. Carefully scoop out the interior with a knife and a grapefruit spoon. Stuff the orange with tea leaves and replace the top. Heat smoker* or covered charcoal or gas grill to a very low temperature, 200 degrees F. (100 C). Place the orange in the smoker and smoke until the orange skin is withered, about 1 hour. Cool. To make tea, blend 1 teaspoon (5 gm) tea with 6 ounces (185 ml) water. Heat to boil. Steep for 5 minutes and add a little honey, if desired.

*If a smoker is not available, bake in over at 200 degrees F (100 C).

Each serving: 5 calories; 00% calories from fat; 00 gm total fat; 00 gm saturated fat; 00 mg cholesterol; 7 mg sodium; 47 mg caffeine.

GERMAN LAYERED TEA

This tea is drunk in East Frisia to ward off the chill of the cold North Sea. Generally, several cups of tea are consumed... dissolving a little of the sugar with each cup.

Serves: 4

Divide rock candy between 4 tea cups. Place tea in a tea pot. Bring water to a near-boil, then pour into tea pot. Steep for 5 minutes. Strain and divide between cups and top with cream.

4 tablespoons (60 gm) rock candy

4 teaspoons (20 gm) black tea leaves

3 cups (740 ml) water

1/2 cup (125 ml) coffee cream

Each serving: 116 calories; 3% calories from fat; 6 gm total fat; 4 gm saturated fat; 20 mg cholesterol; 23 mg sodium; 47 mg caffeine.

INDIAN SPICED TEA

4 teaspoons
(20 gm) black
tea leaves

1 teaspoon
(5 gm) whole
cloves

1 teaspoon
(5 gm) carda-
mom seed or
powder

thin strips of
peel from 1
lemon

3 cups water
(750 ml)

1/4 cup
(60 ml) milk

2 teaspoons
(10 gm) honey

Cardamom is a spice unique to India. It makes a most delicious tea.

Serves: 4

Place tea, cloves, cardamom and lemon peel in a teapot. In a separate pot, heat water to a near boil, and add to teapot.

To serve: divide milk and honey between 4 cups. Strain hot tea into cups. Serve immediately.

Each serving: 103 calories; 8% calories from fat; less than 1 gm total fat; less than 1 gm saturated fat; 1 mg cholesterol; 67 mg sodium; 184 mg caffeine.

LEBANESE ORANGE SCENTED TEA

In Lebanon, the teapot is called a "brik". Tea is so popular that it is served to business customers.

Serves: 4

Place tea, aniseed, cinnamon, cloves and orange peel into a brik or teapot. In a separate pot, heat water to a near-boil. Add water to teapot and allow to steep for 5 minutes. Strain into small cups and add honey.

Each serving: 20 calories; 00% calories from fat; 00 gm total fat; 00 gm saturated fat; 00 mg cholesterol; 9 mg sodium; 47 mg caffeine.

4 teaspoons (20 gm) black tea leaves

2 teaspoons (10 gm) aniseed

1 teaspoon (5 gm) cinnamon

1 teaspoon (5 gm) whole cloves

thin slices of orange peel from 1 orange

1-1/2 cups (375 ml) water

2 teaspoons (10 gm) honey

Merry Tea

This is a wonderfully creamy tea that is sure to calm the spirit and satisfy the sweet tooth.

Serves: 4

1/2 cup (120 gm) freshly squeezed lemon juice

3 cups (750 ml) water

4 teaspoons (20 gm) honey

4 teaspoons (20 gm) black tea leaves

2 egg whites, room temperature

3 tablespoons (45 gm) sugar, divided

Blend all but 1 tablespoon lemon juice with water and honey. Heat to a near-boil. Place tea into teapot and add hot water. While the tea steeps, preheat broiler. In a small bowl, whisk egg whites until frothy. Add 1 tablespoon sugar, a little at a time continuing to whisk until soft peaks form the meringue.

Strain and divide tea into 4 oven proof cups. Top with meringue. Place 6 inches from the boiler and allow meringue to brown. Meanwhile beat remaining lemon juice with remaining sugar. When meringue has browned, remove from oven and allow to cool slightly. Drizzle lemon sugar over meringue.

Each serving: 74 calories; 00% calories from fat; 00 gm total fat; 00 gm saturated fat; 00 mg cholesterol; 35 mg sodium; 47 mg caffeine.

Contemporary Herb Tea

Plan a tea celebration to honor an old friend, an infirmed neighbor, or a health conscious loved one. Spend the afternoon in important talk with a contemporary tea set, delicious glazed lemon cake...and a tiny wrapped gift.

Photo Credits

Tea pot, tray, cups, saucers, creamer and sugar by Debbie Parker/Kuhns and Carl Kuhns provided by Fiori Omni, Cleveland, Ohio 44106. Flatware, Edelstahl's "Rostfrei" provided by Al's Pottery, Cleveland, Ohio 44124. Backdrop "Amazon Terrace," mixed media painting by Donna Morris.

Recipe Credits

A California Cup, recipe page 83
Glazed Lemon Cakes, recipe page 184

MOROCCAN MINT TEA WITH ORANGE BLOSSOMS

Orange blossoms may be found in tea shops, in health food stores, in gourmet stores and in some large supermarkets. This is a lovely scented tea. In Morocco, each guest is expected to drink 3 cups!

Serves: 4

A little hot water

4 teaspoons (20 gm) green tea leaves

1/4 cup (60 gm) dried or fresh mint leaves

4 teaspoons (20 gm) honey

3 cups (750 ml) water

Swish the teapot with a little hot water to warm the pot and to help tea leaves to adhere to the pot. Empty water. Add tea leaves, mint, orange blossoms and honey. In a separate pot, heat water to a near-boil. Pour into the tea pot and allow to steep for 5 minutes. Strain and serve immediately.

Each serving: 24 calories; 00% calories from fat; 00 gm total fat; 00 gm saturated fat; 00 mg cholesterol; 7 mg sodium; 47 mg caffeine.

Mulled Tea

4 cups (1 liter) water

1 large piece cheesecloth

1/2 cup (120 gm) dried fruits (apricots, raisins, dates, currents, figs)

2 teaspoons (10 gm) whole cloves

1/2 teaspoon (3 gm) powdered mace

thin slices of peel from 1 orange

thin slices of fresh ginger

2 tablespoons (15 gm) black tea leaves

Delicious...and a great way to use leftover dried fruits and spices.

Serves: 6

In a medium-sized saucepan, heat water until it is a near-boil. Meanwhile, tie dried fruit, cloves, mace, orange, ginger and tea leaves into the cheese-cloth square allowing for expansion room. When water is hot, place bag in pot, cover and remove from heat. Allow to steep for 5 minutes. Strain and serve immediately.

Each serving: 42 calories; less than 1% calories from fat; 00 gm total fat; 00 gm saturated fat; 00 mg cholesterol; 11 mg sodium; 47 mg caffeine.

ORANGE SPICED ENGLISH TEA

This is a tea which is commonly used for high or low tea. It is delicious when served with a little warm milk.

Serves: 4

In a teapot, blend tea with cloves and orange peel. In a separate pot, heat water to boiling. Pour into teapot. Steep for 3 to 5 minutes (shorter steeping time will make weaker tea with less caffeine). Strain into cups and serve.

4 teaspoons (20 gm) orange pekoe tea leaves

1 teaspoon (5 gm) whole cloves

thin slices of orange peel from 1 orange

4 cups (1 liter) water

Each serving: 4 calories; 00% calories from fat; 00 gm total fat; 00 gm saturated fat; 00 mg cholesterol; 8 mg sodium; 47 mg caffeine.

Popcorn Tea

1/4 cup
(60 gm) raw
brown rice

4 teaspoons
(20 gm) green
tea leaves

3 cups
(750 ml) water

2 teaspoons
(10 gm) honey

A traditional Japanese tea made with roasted rice, this tea takes on a roasted flavor. And the rice may pop during the roasting!

Serves: 4

In a small skillet over low heat, brown and toast rice. This will take only about 15 minutes. During the last 3 minutes add tea leaves. In a medium sized saucepan, heat water to a boil. Add rice and tea. Lower heat to a simmer and simmer for 15 minutes. Strain into tea cups. Add honey and serve.

Each serving: 56 calories; 5% calories from fat; less than 1 gm total fat; 00 gm saturated fat; 00 mg cholesterol; 8 mg sodium; 47 mg caffeine.

RUSSIAN TEA

Traditionally made in a samovar, this tea is made in the morning and served all day.

Serves: 4

In a small saucepan, heat 1 cup (250 ml) water to boiling. Add tea. In a larger saucepan, heat remaining water to a boil. Cover with a flat lid.

When water boils, place 1/4 cup (60 ml) strained tea water into a tea cup. Fill with hot water. Serve remaining tea in the same way or reduce heat of the boiling water, place the small pan of tea on the top of water to warm until ready to drink.

1 cup (250 ml) water

2 teaspoons (5 gm) black tea

3 cups (750 ml) water

Each serving: 2 calories; 00% calories from fat; 00 gm total fat; 00 gm saturated fat; 00 mg cholesterol; 7 mg sodium; 47 mg caffeine.

SPICED ETHIOPIAN TEA

1 teaspoon
(5 gm) carda-
mom seed

1 teaspoon
(5 gm) whole
cloves

1 small piece
cinnamon stick

4 teaspoons
(20 gm) black
tea leaves

2 cups
(500 ml) water

In Ethiopia, tea is consumed in small cups or bowls. It is a strong brew.

Serves: 4

Place cardamom seeds, cloves, cinnamon and tea leaves in a teapot. In a separate pot, heat water to a near-boil and pour into tea pot. Steep for 5 minutes. Strain into cups.

Each serving: 7 calories; less than 1% calories from fat; less than 1 gm total fat; 00 gm saturated fat; 00 mg cholesterol; 9 mg sodium; 47 mg caffeine.

TEA FOR A GROUP

It is senseless to serve inferior-quality tea bags just because it's a large group. Make a cheesecloth tea infuser, put in some really great teas...guests will simply love the tea.

Serves: 25

4-1/2 quarts (4-1/2 liters) of water

1 large piece of cheesecloth

1/2 cup (125 mg) black, green or oolong tea leaves (or a blend)

In a large pot, heat water until it is a near-boil. Meanwhile, tie tea leaves into the cheesecloth square allowing room for expansion. When water is hot, place bag in pot, cover and remove from heat. Allow to steep for 5 minutes. Pour into teapots and serve or ladle from the large pot.

Each serving: 2 calories; 00% calories from fat; 00 gm total fat; 00 gm saturated fat; 00 mg cholesterol; 7 mg sodium; 47 mg caffeine.

HERB TEAS

By definition, Herb Teas are not teas as they do not evolve from the Camellia plant. They may be more properly defined as Herb Infusions.

Herbal infusions go back 4500 years to ancient Chinese, Indian and Japanese culture and healing. Herbal infusions were used, by this time, not so much as a beverage of choice but for healing purposes. There's a story from The Book of Tea & Herbs (see reference in the Bibliography) about an Indian medical student. After studying for seven years, his master told him to go out and "bring back all the plants that have no medicinal value." The student went out and searched the country side for days. He came back with nothing. He explained that "All plants have healing power." His master said, "Go; you are now ready to be a physician."

For this small section of herbal infusions, the concentration will be on the herbs that are delicious in hot brews and that are readily available in tea shops, in health food stores, in gourmet shops or in supermarkets. Proper brewing of herbal infusions begins with the proper preparation as outlined in Chapter 2. However, there are several variations: whenever possible, start with the whole leaf of the herb so there is more surface and more volatile oil. For richer flavor allow the herbs to steep a total of 10 minutes or boil the herbs in water for 10 to 20 minutes reducing the water by half. This will also increase the flavors of the brew.

What herbs should be used? Herbal infusions are properly defined as non-woody plants that die down to the ground after flowering. For tea recipes in this book, we will include certain spices, roots, flowers and seeds. Recipes in this section have been selected because they are delicious and easy to make, with ingredients that the reader will find readily available.

Herb teas may be prepared in advance, cooled and reheated.

MERICAN COZY TEA

1/4 cup (60 gm)
fresh mint
leaves

1 whole nut-
meg, cracked

1 tablespoon
(15 gm) whole
cloves

thinly sliced
peel of 1 lemon

2 teaspoons
(10 gm) honey

3 cups (750 ml)
water

*All the fragrance imaginable...great to
sip in front of a fire.*

Serves: 4

Place mint leaves, nutmeg, cloves,
lemon and honey in a teapot. In a
separate pot, heat water to a near-boil
and pour into pot. Steep for 5 minutes.
Strain into cups.

Each serving: 20 calories; 1% calories from fat; 1 gm
total fat; less than 1 gm saturated fat; 00 mg
cholesterol; 4 mg sodium; 00 mg caffeine.

CALIFORNIA CUP

...sweet, with a hint of California red-woods.

Serves: 4

Place rosemary, chamomile, honey and fennel in a teapot. In a separate pot, heat water to a near-boil and pour into pot. Steep for 10 minutes. Strain into cups.

Each serving: 22 calories; 57% calories from fat; less than 1 gm total fat; 00 gm saturated fat; 00 mg cholesterol; 1 mg sodium; 00 mg caffeine.

2 teaspoons (10 gm) rosemary

2 teaspoons (10 gm) dried chamomile flowers or 1/2 teaspoon (3 gm) natural chamomile oil

2 teaspoons (10 gm) honey

1 tablespoon (15 gm) fennel seed

3 cups (750 ml) water

BLENDED BERRY

1/4 cup
(60 gm) fresh
raspberries

4 teaspoons
(20 gm) fresh
lemongrass

4 teaspoons
(20 gm) dried
rose petals

1 small stick
cinnamon

2 teaspoons
(10 gm) honey

3 cups (750
ml) water

Using fresh berries in tea is a great idea: it adds color, subtle flavor and a nice after taste. Raspberries are used here...feel free to substitute strawberries or blueberries.

Serves: 4

In a small bowl, crush raspberries with the back of a fork. Place raspberries, lemongrass, rose petals, cinnamon and honey in a teapot. In a separate pot, heat water to a near-boil and pour into pot. Steep for 10 minutes. Strain into cups.

Each serving:00 calories; 00% calories from fat; 00 gm total fat; 00 gm saturated fat; 00 mg cholesterol; 00 mg sodium; 00 mg caffeine.

Blossom Bloomer

Blossoms for this delicious tea are available at many tea shops. Or, they may be replaced with natural chamomile or lavender oils.

Serves: 4

Place chamomile, lavender, and honey in teapot. In a separate pot, heat water to a near-boil and pour into pot. Steep for 10 minutes. Strain into cups.

Each serving: 38 calories; 00% calories from fat; 00 gm total fat; 00 gm saturated fat; 00 mg cholesterol; 1 mg sodium; 00 mg caffeine.

4 teaspoons (20 gm) dried chamomile flowers or 1 teaspoon (5 gm) natural chamomile oil

4 teaspoons (20 gm) dried lavender flowers or 1 teaspoon (5 gm) natural lavender oil

1 teaspoon (5 gm) honey

2 cups (500 ml) water

CHRISTMAS DELIGHT

2 dried bay
leaves

2 teaspoons
(10 gm) dried
juniper berries

1 large sprig
fresh rosemary

2 teaspoons
(10 gm) fresh
mint

1 teaspoon
(5 gm) honey

1 teaspoon
(5 gm) whole
cloves

3 cups
(750 ml) water

The aroma of this tea is reminiscent of Christmas trees. If juniper berries are not readily available, try a drop or 2 of juniper oil.

Serves: 4

Place bay leaves, juniper berries, rosemary, mint, honey and cloves in a teapot. In a separate pot, heat water to a near-boil and pour into pot. Steep for 10 minutes. Strain into cups.

Each serving: 8 calories; 00% calories from fat; 00 gm total fat; 00 gm saturated fat; 00 mg cholesterol; 1 mg sodium; 00 mg caffeine.

EUROPEAN BLEND

...an aroma which will bring you back thoughts of the "old country."

Serves: 2

Place nutmeg, cinnamon, lemon balm and honey in a teapot. In a separate pot, heat water to a near-boil and pour into pot. Steep for 10 minutes. Strain into cups.

Each serving: 23 calories; 2% calories from fat; 00 gm total fat; 00 gm saturated fat; 00 mg cholesterol; 1 mg sodium; 00 mg caffeine.

1 teaspoon (5 gm) nutmeg

2 teaspoons (10 gm) cinnamon

1 tablespoon (15 gm) fresh lemon balm or mint leaves

1 teaspoon (5 gm) honey

2 cups (500 ml) water

E XOTIC HERBAL

4 cups (1 liter) water

1 small stick cinnamon

1 teaspoon (5 gm) cardamom seeds

2 teaspoons (10 gm) fenugreek (ground or seed)

1 small dried hibiscus flower

1 teaspoon (5 gm) honey

Here is a sweetly flavored tea with a touch of the exotic.

Serves: 4

Place water into a medium-sized saucepan. Add cinnamon, cardamom, fenugreek, hibiscus and honey. Heat to a boil, reduce heat and simmer for 15 minutes until the tea is reduced to 3 cups. Strain into cups and serve immediately.

Each serving: 14 calories; less than 1% calories from fat; less than 1 gm total fat; 00 gm saturated fat; 00 mg cholesterol; 1 mg sodium; 00 mg caffeine.

Venetian Tea

O solo mio...with this zany tea ceremony. For this tea...different is the key...unusual cups, deco pot. Invite the funniest people you know and sing some old (possibly Italian?) songs.

Photo Credits
Venetian Mille Fliori cups and saucers provided by Donna Morris. Russell Wright Tea Set, c. 1940, provided by Affordable Antiques, Lakewood, Ohio 44107. Acrylic surface crafted by Jeff Dube.

Recipe Credits
Warmed Mint Comforter Tea, recipe page 98
Banana Swirl Tea Rolls, recipe page 170

GINGER BLEND

Of the herbs used in tea, ginger is, by far, the most potent. It beautifully carries the delicate flavors of the other ingredients.

Serves: 4

Place water in a medium-sized saucepan. Add ginger root, rose hips, aniseed, honey and cloves. Bring to a boil, reduce heat and simmer for 15 minutes. Strain into cups and serve immediately.

Each serving:10 calories; less than 1% calories from fat; less than 1 gm total fat; 00 gm saturated fat; 00 mg cholesterol; 2 mg sodium; 00 mg caffeine.

4 cups (1 liter) water

4 thin slices of ginger root

2 teaspoons (10 gm) crushed dried rose hips

1 teaspoon (5 gm) aniseed

1 teaspoon (5 gm) honey

1 teaspoon (5 gm) whole cloves

ORANGE UPLIFTER

3 cups (750 ml) water

1/4 teaspoon (1 gm) dried licorice root or 3 slices fresh fennel bulb

1 teaspoon (5 gm) caraway seed

thin strips of orange peel from 1 orange

1 teaspoon (5 gm) honey

2 teaspoons (10 gm) dried catnip (or mint)

The fragrance of this tea is wonderful. Just a little of this tea will uplift and revitalize.

Serves: 2

Heat water in a medium-sized saucepan. Add licorice, caraway seed, orange, honey and catnip. Simmer for 15 minutes allowing brew to reduce to 2 cups (500 ml). Strain into cups and serve immediately.

Each serving: 18 calories; less than 1% calories from fat; less than 1 gm total fat; 00 gm saturated fat; 00 mg cholesterol; 1 mg sodium; 00 mg caffeine.

PEPPERED SPEARMINT DELIGHT

...a hint of root beer in this tea.

Serves: 2

Place sarsaparilla, mint, peppercorns and honey in a teapot. In a separate pot, heat water to a near-boil and pour into pot. Steep for 10 minutes. Strain into cups.

Each serving:24 calories; less than 1% calories from fat; less than 1 gm total fat; 00 gm saturated fat; 00 mg cholesterol; 1 mg sodium; 00 mg caffeine.

1 tablespoon (15 gm) dried sarsaparilla root or a drop or two of sarsparilla oil

2 teaspoons (10 gm) fresh mint leaves

8 green or black pepper-corns, crushed

2 teaspoons (10 gm) honey

2 cups (500 ml) water

ROSE REFRESHER

This tea is fragrant and refreshing.

Serves: 4

4 teaspoon (20 gm) dried rose petals

2 teaspoons (10 gm) crushed dried rose hips

2 teaspoons (10 gm) dried sage leaves

1 small dried hibiscus flower

1 teaspoon (5 gm) honey

4 cups (1 liter) water

Place rose petals, rose hips, sage, hibiscus and honey in a teapot. In a separate pot, heat water to a near-boil and pour into pot. Steep for 10 minutes. Strain into cups.

Each serving: 6 calories; less than 1% calories from fat; less than 1 gm total fat; 00 gm saturated fat; 00 mg cholesterol; 00 mg sodium; 00 mg caffeine.

DOUBLE MINT TEA

...a lovely minty flavored beverage.

Serves: 2

Place mint leaves, lemon balm, rosemary and honey in a teapot. In a separate pot, heat water to a near-boil and pour into pot. Steep for 10 minutes. Strain into cups.

Each serving:31 calories; 00% calories from fat; l00 gm total fat; 00 gm saturated fat; 00 mg cholesterol; 00 mg sodium; 00 mg caffeine.

1 teaspoon (5 gm) spearmint leaves

1 teaspoon (5 gm) mint leaves

2 teaspoons (10 gm) lemon balm

1 small sprig fresh rosemary

1 teaspoon (5 gm) honey

2 cups (500 ml) water

MEDICINAL TEAS

Does tea have medicinal qualities? Throughout centuries, whole studies have devoted time and energy into the research of the medicinal qualities of teas. Certainly, hot liquid goes far to relieve many symptoms. So...take relief with the following teas for coughs, colds and flu.

HOT LEMONADE

Great for relieving congestion, this tea is also delicious.

Serves: 2

Pour water into a medium-sized saucepan. Add remaining ingredients and bring to a boil. Cover and steep for 10 minutes. Strain and drink immediately.

Each serving: 31 calories; less than 1% calories from fat; less than 1 gm total fat; 1 gm saturated fat; 00 mg cholesterol; 7 mg sodium; 22 mg caffeine.

2 cups (500 ml) water

the juice of 1 lemon

3 slices fresh ginger

2 teaspoons (10 gm) honey

1/4 teaspoon (1 gm) cayenne pepper

2 teaspoons (10 gm) green tea leaves

L ICORICE RELAXER

This special tea is warm and comforting.

Serves: 2

2 cups (500 ml) water

a few drops (1 ml) licorice oil

2 teaspoons (10 gm) dried chamomile

flowers or a few drops (1 ml) natural chamomile oil

2 teaspoons (10 gm) green tea leaves

Pour water into a medium-sized saucepan. Add remaining ingredients and heat to a boil. Cover and steep for 10 minutes. Strain and drink immediately.

Each serving: 5 calories; 4% calories from fat; less than 1 gm total fat; 00 gm saturated fat; 00 mg cholesterol; 7 mg sodium; 22 mg caffeine.

Sage Sipper

This tea is very effective at alleviating cold symptoms. If possible, find large, fresh sage leaves, fresh hyssop and thyme. Dry in 200 degree F (100 C) oven for 1 hour.

Serves: 2

Pour water into a medium-sized saucepan. Add remaining ingredients and heat to a boil. Cover and steep for 10 minutes. Strain and drink immediately.

Each serving: 7 calories; less than 1 % calories from fat; less than 1 gm total fat; 00 gm saturated fat; 00 mg cholesterol; 8 mg sodium; 22 mg caffeine.

2 cups (500 ml) water

sprig fresh sage leaves, dried

2 teaspoons (10 gm) fresh hyssop, dried, or a few drops (1 ml) natural hyssop oil

3 sprigs fresh thyme, dried

2 teaspoons (10 gm) green tea leaves

WARMED MINT COMFORTER

...to warm and comfort.

Serves: 2

2 teaspoons (10 gm) dried mint leaves

2 teaspoons (10 gm) dried rose hips or a few drops (2 ml) natural rose hip oil

2 teaspoons (10 gm) dried sage leaves

2 teaspoons (10 gm) honey

2 teaspoons (10 gm) green tea

2 cups (500 ml) water

Place mint leaves, rose hips, sage, honey and green tea in a teapot. In a separate pot, heat water to a near-boil and pour into pot. Steep for 10 minutes. Strain into cups.

Each serving: 26 calories; less than 1% calories from fat; less than 1 gm total fat; 00 gm saturated fat; 00 mg cholesterol; 8 mg sodium; 22 mg caffeine.

ENERGY GIVING TEA
LEMON LIFTER

Garlic and black tea are the secret ingredients of this energy giving tea.

Serves: 2

Place garlic, lemon juice, honey and black tea in a teapot. In a separate pot, heat water to a near-boil and pour into pot. Steep for 10 minutes. Strain into cups.

Each serving: 32 calories; less than 1 % calories from fat; less than 1 gm total fat; 00 gm saturated fat; 00 mg cholesterol; 8 mg sodium; 47 mg caffeine.

2 cloves garlic

the juice of 1 lemon

2 teaspoons (10 gm) honey

2 teaspoons (10 gm) black tea leaves

2 cups (500 ml) water

ROSEMARY RIVETER

1 large sprig
fresh rosemary
or 1 teaspoon
(5 gm) dried
rosemary

1 teaspoon
(5 gm) fennel
seed

2 teaspoons
(10 gm) honey

2 teaspoons
(10 gm) black
tea leaves

2 cups (500 ml)
water

The ingredients for this stimulating tea can be found in most all kitchens.

Serves: 2

Place rosemary, fennel, honey and black tea in a teapot. In a separate pot, heat water to a near-boil and pour into pot. Steep for 10 minutes. Strain into cups.

Each serving: 31 calories; less than 1% calories from fat; less than 1 gm total fat; 00 gm saturated fat; 00 mg cholesterol; 9 mg sodium; 47 mg caffeine.

PEPPERMINT COCKTAIL

This tea is good for mild indigestion or stomach cramping.

Serves: 2

Heat water in a medium-sized saucepan. Add peppermint, fenugreek, honey and tea leaves. Simmer for 15 minutes allowing brew to reduce to 2 cups (500 ml). Strain into cups and serve immediately.

Each serving: 38 calories; 12% calories from fat; less than 1 gm total fat; less than 1 gm saturated fat; less than 1 mg cholesterol; 3 mg sodium; 22 mg caffeine.

3 cups (750 ml) water

2 teaspoons (10 gm) dried peppermint leaves or a few drops (2 ml) natural peppermint oil or extract

2 teaspoons (10 gm) fenugreek, ground or seeds

1 teaspoon (5 gm) honey

2 teaspoons (10 gm) green tea leaves

GINGER CUBE TEA

3 cups (750 ml)
water

2 tablespoons
(30 gm) ginger
root cut into
small cubes

1 teaspoon
(5 gm) fennel
seed

1 teaspoon
(5 gm) honey

2 teaspoons
(10 gm) green
tea

1 teaspoon (5
gm) basil leaves

*Natural ginger (found in ginger root,
ground ginger and ginger ale) are
wonderful tonics for stomach ailments
such as cramping and motion sickness.
Drink slowly, but enjoy.*

Serves: 2

Heat water in a medium-sized saucepan. Add ginger root, fennel seed,
honey, tea and basil. Simmer for 15
minutes allowing brew to reduce to 2
cups (500 ml). Strain into cups and
serve immediately.

Each serving: 46 calories; 9% calories from fat; less
than 1 gm total fat; less than 1 gm saturated fat; 00
mg cholesterol; 18 mg sodium; 44 mg caffeine.

SLEEPY TEA

...the most effective way to slow down after a long, hectic day.

Serves: 2

Place chamomile, lavender, catnip, honey and green tea in a teapot. In a separate pot, heat water to a near-boil and pour into pot. Steep for 10 minutes. Strain into cups.

Each serving: 33 calories; 27% calories from fat; 1 gm total fat; less than 1 gm saturated fat; 00 mg cholesterol; 8 mg sodium; 22 mg caffeine.

2 teaspoons (10 gm) dried chamomile flowers or a few drops (2 ml) natural chamomile oil

2 teaspoons (10 gm) dried lavender flowers or a few drops (1 ml) natural lavender oil

2 teaspoons (10 gm) dried catnip

2 teaspoons (10 gm) honey

2 teaspoons (10 gm) green tea leaves

2 cups (500 ml) water

Honey and Lemon

the juice of 1
lemon

2 teaspoons
(10 gm) honey

1 garlic clove

2 teaspoons
(10 gm) green
tea

2 cups (500 ml)
water

This tea may be sipped slowly or gargled. It is effective at coating the throat and helps alleviate pain and hoarseness.

Serves: 2

Place lemon juice, honey, garlic and green tea in a teapot. In a separate pot, heat water to a near-boil and pour into pot. Steep for 10 minutes. Strain into cups.

Each serving: 50 calories; 00% calories from fat; 00 gm total fat; 00 gm saturated fat; 00 mg cholesterol; 8 mg sodium; 22 mg caffeine.

Iced Tea Picnic

What could be more American than iced tea...one of the most popular beverages in the world and growing in popularity! For this friendly gathering, assemble the most elegant tall crystal glasses available...using glass stirrers for a delightful "clink." Add flowers and delicious shrimp bruschetta...it is an afternoon delight.

Photo Credits
Czechoslovokian-style striped glasses provided by Affordable Antiques, Lakewood, Ohio 44107. Sasaki "Windows" cutlery provided by Al's Pottery, Lyndhurst, Ohio 44124.

Recipe Credits
Fruited Tea, recipe page 114
Shrimp on Brochetta, recipe page 199

ELDER FLOWER TEA

This tea is both soothing and fragrant.

Serves: 2

Place mint, elderberry, thyme, honey and green tea in a teapot. In a separate pot, heat water to a near-boil and pour into pot. Steep for 10 minutes. Strain into cups.

Each serving: 28 calories; less than 1% calories from fat; less than 1 gm total fat; less than 1 gm saturated fat; 00 mg cholesterol; 8 mg sodium; 22 mg caffeine.

2 teaspoons (10 gm) dried or fresh mint leaves

2 teaspoons (10 gm) dried elderberry flowers or a few drops (2 ml) natural elderberry oil

1 sprig fresh thyme

2 teaspoons (10 gm) honey

2 teaspoons (10 gm) green tea

2 cups (500 ml) water

4 ICED TEAS

Nothing is more American than iced tea. In 1904, Richard Blechynden, a Brit, arrived all the way from Calcutta India, to represent tea-making at the St. Louis Louisiana Purchase Exposition.

Richard brought with him colorfully dressed Sri Lankans to help him promote the fine Ceylon and Indian teas.

The weather turned stifling, humid and hot. Day after day the crowd passed their tea booth in favor of consuming cold and iced drinks. In desperation, Richard tried filling tall glasses with pieces of ice and pouring hot tea into them. Iced tea immediately was a hit...so cooling and refreshing. We know the rest of the story...iced tea became a favorite beverage of the exposition. And...iced tea is the number one beverage in the U.S. and is growing in popularity all around the world.

How to Make the Perfect Iced Tea:

There are two methods:

1. Prepare a double strength batch of regular tea or of any of the tea recipes in this book. Cool slightly, then pour over ice cubes.

2. Place 2 teaspoons (10 gm) per cup (250 ml) of loose tea into a large container. Fill with cold water and allow to set overnight in the refrigerator or in the sun for 1 hour. Strain and pour over ice cubes.

It's a great idea to prepare "tea cubes" to go with the iced brew. Simply pour a favorite hot or iced tea brew into ice cubes trays. Freeze and serve as ice for the beverage. Sugar, mint leaves or lemon juice may be added to taste.

Honey is the perfect sweetner for hot tea. Iced tea, on the other hand, has a delicate taste with a crisp after bite. The perfect sweetener for iced tea is simple syrup.

SIMPLE SYRUP

...the perfect sweetener for iced tea.

Serves: 48, 1 teaspoon (5 gm) servings

In a medium-sized sauce pan, blend sugar with water. Heat to a boil, stirring to dissolve the sugar. When all sugar is dissolved, cool, pour into a sealed container and refrigerate. It will taste good for up to 3 months.

1 cup (250 gm) sugar

1/2 cup (125 ml) water

Each serving: 15 calories; 00% calories from fat; 00 gm total fat; 00 gm saturated fat; 00 mg cholesterol; 00 mg sodium; 00 mg caffeine.

ICED CREAM TEA

4 teaspoons
(20 gm) black
tea leaves

2 cups (500 ml)
water

4 teaspoons
(20 gm) simple
syrup

2 scoops, 1 cup,
(250 gm) vanilla
ice cream or
frozen yogurt

cracked ice to
fill half a
blender cup

I love black tea for this recipe — but green tea (especially Mat-cha) works as well.

Serves: 4

Place tea leaves in a teapot. In a separate pot, heat water to a near-boil and pour into pot. Steep for 5 minutes. Add simple syrup and allow to cool for 1 hour. When ready to serve, fill blender cup with ice cream and cracked ice. Add strained tea mixture and blend on high until mixture is smooth and icy. Pour into 4 tall glasses and serve.

Each serving, made with non-fat frozen yogurt: 40 calories; 00% calories from fat; 00 gm total fat; 00 gm saturated fat; 00 mg cholesterol; 32 mg sodium; 47 mg caffeine.

I CED SODA TEA

Any soda may be used, but root beer is excellent.

Serves: 4

Place tea leaves in a teapot. In a separate pot, heat water to a near-boil and pour into pot. Steep for 5 minutes. Add simple syrup and allow to cool for 1 hour. When ready to serve, fill blender cup with ice cream, root beer or other soda and cracked ice. Add strained tea mixture and blend on high until mixture is smooth and icy. Pour into 4 tall glasses and enjoy.

Each serving, made with non-fat yogurt: 67 calories; 00% calories from fat; 00 gm total fat; 00 gm saturated fat; 00 mg cholesterol; 41 mg sodium; 47 mg caffeine.

4 teaspoons (20 gm) black tea leaves

1 cup (250 ml) water

4 teaspoons (20 gm) simple syrup

2 scoops, 1 cup, (250 gm) vanilla ice cream or frozen yogurt

1 cup, (250 ml) root beer or other flavored soda

cracked ice to fill half a blender cup

FRUITED TEA

4 teaspoons
(20 gm) black
tea leaves

2 cups (500 ml)
water

1 cup (250 ml)
orange, pine-
apple or apple
juice

2 teaspoons
(10 gm) simple
syrup

ice

mint leaves for
garnish

Try orange, pineapple or apple juice...or a blend...for this tasty treat.

Serves: 4

Place tea leaves in a teapot. In a separate pot, heat water to a near-boil and pour into pot. Steep for 5 minutes. Add juice and simple syrup. Strain into tall glasses which have been filled with ice. Garnish with mint leaves.

Each serving: 39 calories; less than 1% calories from fat; less than 1 gm total fat; less than 1 gm saturated fat; 00 mg cholesterol; 9 mg sodium; 47 mg caffeine.

LEMONADE TEA

Minty and refreshing.

Serves: 2

Place tea leaves and mint leaves in a teapot. In a separate pot, heat water to a near-boil and pour into pot. Steep for 5 minutes. Add lemon, simple syrup and lemon juice. Strain into tall glasses which have been filled with ice. Garnish with mint leaves.

Each serving: 21 calories; 00% calories from fat; 00 gm total fat; 00 gm saturated fat; 00 mg cholesterol; 8 mg sodium; 47 mg caffeine.

2 teaspoons (10 gm) black tea leaves

2 tablespoons (30 gm) fresh mint leaves

2 cups (500 ml) water

2 teaspoons (10 gm) simple syrup

juice of 1 lemon

ice

mint leaves for garnish

P EACHY ICED TEA

What a lovely blend of flavors.

Serves: 4

4 teaspoons (20 gm) black tea leaves

2 tablespoons (30 gm) fresh mint leaves

3 cups (750 ml) water

4 teaspoons (20 gm) simple syrup

2 small peaches, peeled, seeded and chopped

ice

mint leaves for garnish

Place tea leaves and mint leaves in a teapot. In a separate pot, heat water to a near-boil and pour into pot. Steep for 5 minutes. Add simple syrup. Strain into a pitcher and add peaches. Fill pitcher with ice. Allow flavors to blend for 5 minutes, then serve in tall glasses.

Each serving: 36 calories; less than 1% calories from fat; less than 1 gm total fat; less than 1 gm saturated fat; 00 mg cholesterol; 7 mg sodium; 47 mg caffeine.

PINEAPPLE PLEASER

A taste of the tropics.

Serves: 4

Place tea leaves and mint leaves in a teapot. In a separate pot, heat water to a near-boil and pour into pot. Steep for 5 minutes. Add simple syrup and allow to cool for 1 hour. When ready to serve, fill blender cup with pineapple tidbits and cracked ice. Add strained tea mixture and blend on high until mixture is smooth and icy. Pour into 4 tall glasses and garnish with mint leaves.

Each serving: 50 calories; less than 1% calories from fat; less than 1 gm total fat; less than 1 gm saturated fat; 00 mg cholesterol; 8 mg sodium; 47 mg caffeine.

4 teaspoons (20 gm) black tea leaves

2 tablespoons (30 gm) fresh mint leaves

3 cups (750 ml) water

4 teaspoons (20 gm) simple syrup

1 cup (250 gm) pineapple tidbits with syrup

cracked ice to fill half a blender cup

mint leaves for garnish

TROPICAL TEA FRAPPE

4 teaspoons
(20 gm) black
tea leaves

2 cups (500 ml)
water

4 teaspoons
(20 gm) simple
syrup

cracked ice to
fill half a
blender cup

thin twists of
lemon peel for
garnish

This is a different twist on iced tea.

Serves: 4

Place tea leaves in a teapot. In a separate pot, heat water to a near-boil and pour into pot. Steep for 5 minutes. Add simple syrup and allow to cool for 1 hour. When ready to serve, fill blender cup halfway with cracked ice. Add strained tea mixture and blend on high until mixture is smooth and icy. Pour into 4 tall glasses and garnish with lemon twists.

Each serving: 17 calories; 00% calories from fat; 00 gm total fat; 00 gm saturated fat; 00 mg cholesterol; 8 mg sodium; 47 mg caffeine.

FLAVORED ICED TEA FOR A GROUP

A delicious punch...use tea flavored ice cubes or an ice ring made from double strength tea and mint leaves

Serves: 24

In a medium-sized saucepan, bring 4 cups water to a near-boil. Stir in tea. Cover and allow to steep for 5 minutes. Strain into a 6-quart punch bowl. Add cold water. Stir in lemonade and limeade concentrates, cranberry juice and ginger ale. Garnish with orange and lemon slices.

Each serving: 68 calories; less than 1% calories from fat; less than 1 gm total fat; less than 1 gm saturated fat; 00 mg cholesterol; 7 mg sodium; 10 mg caffeine.

4 cups (1 liter) water

1/2 cup (125 gm) green or black tea leaves

2 cups (500 ml) cold water

2 cans, 6 ounces each (185 ml each) frozen concentrated lemonade

2 cans, 6 ounces each (185 ml each) frozen concentrated limeade

2 cups (500 ml) cranberry juice

2 bottles (2 liters each) ginger ale

orange and lemon slices for garnish

Evening Spirits Tea

For a romantic interlude, try a tea nightcap paired with make-ahead snacks. For this midnight tea party, use the most elegant tea set available, light plenty of candles, and let the good times roll.

Photo Credits
China, Mitsu-Gosni 3 Star made in Japan c. 1920, provided by Donna Morris. Hand crocheted tablecloth and fork provided by Mary Ward. Gold flatware Retroneu "Kimberly" and Villeray & Boch "Quartet" and "Pisa" candlesticks provided by Al's Pottery, Lyndhurst, Ohio 44124.

Recipe Credits
Tea Nightcap, recipe page 132
Egg Salad with Capers on Polenta, recipe page 190
Snow Peas with Cheese and Herbs, recipe page 193

5 TEA WITH SPIRITS

Tea blends well with alcohol and spirits. Traditionally, it has been used in alcohol based punches, toddies, spiced drinks and rum drinks. You have your choice of teas...select black for more caffeine, green for less.

To reduce the alcoholic content of these drinks, bring the tea water to a full boil, add the alcohol and boil alcohol with the tea water for about 5 minutes.

Try AFTER DINNER TEA which is simply 6 ounces (180 ml) of a favorite tea blended with 1 ounce (30 ml) of favorite liqueur. Simple syrup, honey or milk may be added.

Try a HOT SHOT: add a touch of hot tea to a favorite liqueur to warm it up.

Or try one of these delicious recipes for tea with spirits.

BRANDIED TEA PUNCH

This is a sparkling and bubbly punch.

Serves: 25

4 cups (1 liter) water

1/4 cup (60 gm) black or green tea leaves

1/2 cup (125 ml) brandy

1 liter club soda, chilled

1 fifth (750 ml) sparkling bur-gundy, chilled

1/2 cup (125 gm) simple syrup (recipe page 111)

In a medium sized sauce pan, heat water to a rolling boil. Add tea, cover and remove from heat. Steep for 5 minutes. Cool. In a large punch bowl, blend strained tea with brandy, club soda, sparkling burgundy and simple syrup. Serve immediately.

Each serving: 37 calories; 00% calories from fat; 00 gm total fat; 00 gm saturated fat; 00 mg cholesterol; 13 mg sodium; 23 mg caffeine.

ENGLISH FLAMING TEA CUP

This tea is most unusual.

Serves: 4

Place tea in a teapot. In a separate pot, heat water to a near-boil and pour into pot. Steep for 10 minutes. Preheat oven to 350 degrees F (175 C). Stud orange with whole cloves. Place on a flat heat proof dish and pour 2 tablespoons corn syrup over it. Place it in the oven for 15 minutes to lightly brown. Remove, cool and cut into quarters. Place in a medium-sized saucepan with remaining corn syrup, port and strained tea. Simmer for 15 minutes. Divide amount between 4 heat proof tea cups. Heat rum, pour into cup and carefully ignite.

Each serving: 179 calories; less than 1% calories from fat; less than 1 gm total fat; less than 1 gm saturated fat; 00 mg cholesterol; 18 mg sodium; 24 mg caffeine.

2 teaspoons (10 gm) black or green tea leaves

2 cups (500 ml) water

1 whole orange

1 teaspoon (5 gm) whole cloves

3 tablespoons (45 gm) corn syrup

1 cup (250 ml) tawny port

2 ounces (30 ml) Jamaican rum

FRAPPE de MENTHE

...a smooth, and cooling dessert.

Serves: 4

2 teaspoons (10 gm) black tea leaves

1/4 cup (60 gm) confectioners sugar

2 cups (500 ml) water

1/4 cup (60 ml) white creme de menthe

1/4 cup (60 ml) white creme de cacao

mint sprigs for garnish

Place tea and confectioners sugar in a teapot. In a separate pan, heat water to a near-boil and pour into pot. Steep for 10 minutes. Strain into a mixing bowl. Blend with remaining ingredients except mint sprigs. Pour into ice cube trays without dividers and freeze until firm. Just before serving, empty mixture into a medium sized mixing bowl. With an electric mixer, beat until the frappe is smooth and blended. Serve in stemmed dessert glasses garnished with a mint leaf.

Each serving: 131 calories; less than 1% calories from fat; less than 1 gm total fat; less than 1 gm saturated fat; 00 mg cholesterol; 5 mg sodium; 24 mg caffeine.

HOT BUTTERED TEA

...a smooth and richly flavored treat.

Serves: 2

Place tea, cloves and simple syrup in a teapot. In a separate pot, heat water to a near-boil and pour into pot. Steep for 10 minutes. Strain into cups. Pour 1 ounce rum into each cup, top with a pat of butter and a cinnamon stick stirrer.

Each serving: 136 calories; 30% calories from fat; 5 gm total fat; 3 gm saturated fat; 11 mg cholesterol; 54 mg sodium; 47 mg caffeine.

2 teaspoons (10 gm) black or green tea leaves

2 teaspoons (10 gm) whole cloves

2 teaspoons (10 gm) simple syrup (recipe on page 111)

1-1/2 cups (375 ml) water

2 ounces (60 ml) light rum

2 teaspoons (10 gm) butter

2 cinnamon sticks

IRISH TEA

2 teaspoons
(10 gm) black or
green tea leaves

1 teaspoon
(5 gm) whole
cloves

1 teaspoon
(5 gm) ground
allspice

2 teaspoons
(10 gm) simple
syrup (recipe on
page 111)

1 nutmeg,
cracked

1-1/2 cups
(375 ml) water

2 ounces (60 ml)
Irish whiskey

2 tablespoons
(60 gm) freshly
whipped cream

2 cinnamon
sticks

It is the opinion of the author, that this drink has far more flavor than its coffee counterpart. Try it and see!

Serves: 2

Place tea, cloves, allspice, simple syrup and nutmeg in a teapot. In a separate pot, heat water to a near-boil and pour into pot. Steep for 10 minutes. Strain into cups. Pour 1 ounce Irish whiskey into each cup. Top with whipped cream. Stir with a cinnamon stick stirrer.

Each serving: 158 calories; 35% calories from fat; 6 gm total fat; 4 gm saturated fat; 20 mg cholesterol; 17 mg sodium; 47 mg caffeine.

JAMAICAN TEA PUNCH

This is a sipping punch!

Serves: 6

Place tea in a teapot. In a separate pot, heat water to a near-boil and pour into pot. Steep for 10 minutes. Strain into a medium saucepan and add remaining ingredients. Heat to a near-boil and serve.

Each serving: 80 calories; 00% calories from fat; 00 gm total fat; 161 gm saturated fat; 00 mg cholesterol; 3 mg sodium; 65 mg caffeine.

2 teaspoons (10 gm) black tea

4 cups (1 liter) water

1/4 cup (60 ml) Jamaican rum (light)

1/4 cup (60 ml) brandy

1/4 cup (60 ml) Curacao

juice of 2 lemons

PLANTERS PUNCH

8 cups (2 liters) water

3 tablespoons (45 gm) black tea leaves

1 cup (250 ml) dark Jamaican rum

1 cup (250 ml) curacao

6 oz. (185 ml) frozen pineapple concentrate, defrosted

6 oz. (185 ml) frozen orange juice concentrate, defrosted

6 oz. (185 ml) frozen limeade concentrate, defrosted

12 oz. (375 ml) frozen lemonade concentrate

cracked ice

pineapple chunks, orange slices, strawberries and maraschino cherries

Planters punch traditionally has a very high alcohol content. This lightened version is delicious and has less than 1 ounce alcohol per serving.

Serves: 20

Heat water to a near-boil in a large saucepan. Add tea, cover and remove from heat. Allow to steep for 5 minutes. Strain into a large pitcher or serving bowl. Add remaining ingredients, stirring well. Fill tall glasses 2/3 full of ice. Ladle in punch and garnish with fruit.

Each serving: 168 calories; 00% calories from fat; 00 gm total fat; 00 gm saturated fat; 00 mg cholesterol; 4 mg sodium; 21 mg caffeine.

TEA LIQUEUR

...very strong tea combined with spirits.

Serves: 15

Place tea in a teapot. In a separate pot, heat water to a near-boil and pour into first pot. Steep for 5 minutes. Strain into a mixing bowl. Cool and blend with simple syrup and vodka. Store in a clean container. Liqueur will be ready for drinking in 2 weeks.

Each serving: 65 calories; 00% calories from fat; 00 gm total fat; 00 gm saturated fat; 00 mg cholesterol; 7 mg sodium; 47 mg caffeine.

5 tablespoons (75 gm) black, green or jasmine tea leaves

1 cup (250 ml) water

1/2 cup (125 ml) simple syrup (recipe on page 111)

1 cup (250 ml) vodka

TEA NIGHTCAP

...a true sleepy time tea.

Serves: 2

1 teaspoon
(5 gm) green
tea leaves

2 teaspoons
(10 gm)
simple syrup
(recipe on
page 111)

1-1/2 cups
(375 ml) water

2 ounces
(60 ml)
Frangelico
liqueur

1 cup (250 ml)
milk, warmed

Place tea and simple syrup in a teapot.
In a separate pot, heat water to a
near-boil and pour into pot. Steep for
10 minutes. Strain into cups. Pour 1
ounce Frangelico into each cup. Add
warm milk.

Each serving: 165 calories; less than 1% calories from
fat; less than 1 gm total fat; less than 1 gm saturated
fat; 2 mg cholesterol; 67 mg sodium; 24 mg caffeine.

TEA TODDY

...for the brandy lover

Serves: 2

Place tea, cloves, cinnamon stick, simple syrup and nutmeg in a teapot. In a separate pot, heat water to a near-boil and pour into pot. Steep for 10 minutes. Strain into cups. Pour 1 ounce brandy into each cup. Serve immediately.

Each serving: 121 calories; 5% calories from fat; 1 gm total fat; less than 1 gm saturated fat; 00 mg cholesterol; 10 mg sodium; 47 mg caffeine.

2 teaspoons (10 gm) black or green tea leaves

1 teaspoon (5 gm) whole cloves

1 cinnamon stick

2 teaspoons (10 gm) simple syrup (recipe on page 111)

1 nutmeg, cracked

1-1/2 cups (375 ml) water

2 ounces (60 ml) brandy

6 TEA CEREMONIES & TRADITIONS

Nursery Tea

What child, aged 4 to 40, does not love a tea party? We have invited our friends Hans and Mary to visit. Hans takes his pet dog Spot with him wherever he goes....and Mary has her doll Gilda. When planning nursery tea, use "dress ups": bring out the old dolls, set the table, and watch the children beam. A suggestion: use plenty of milk and sugar in the Cambric tea, and serve child sized portions of cinnamon bears, snickerdoodle coins, and mini muffins.

Photo Credits

Japanese Luster Ware Tea Set, c. 1920, provided by The Wabi Shop, Cleveland, Ohio 44106. 21-inch boy doll (Hans) Kammer and Reinhart, 114, glass eyes, sleep. 23-1/2 inch girl doll (Mary) Heinrick Handwerk Simon & Halbig, sleep eyes, genuine hair and eyebrows. 8 inch small doll (Gilda) Kammer and Reinhart, 114, painted eyes. Dolls, doll accessories, doll table and chairs provided by Jane Moody.

Recipe Credits

Cambric Tea, recipe page 154
Cinnamon Toast Bears, recipe page 155
Cookie Smile Snickerdoodles, recipe page 156
Cranberry Mini Muffins, recipe page 153

HOW TO READ TEA LEAVES

"Matrons, who toss the cup, and see the grounds of fate in grounds of tea..." From The Tea Book (see reference in Bibliography).

In tea leaf reading, or tasseography, the tea cup is mapped and read according to configurations formed by wet tea leaves. Here's how:

1) The tea leaf reader ("reader") makes a cup for the tea drinker, the person with a question ("questioner"). The questioner drinks the tea, leaving enough tea in the bottom of the cup to cover the tea leaves.

2) The questioner picks up the cup by its handle and swirls the tea three times to his left. He then turns the cup upside down with the handle directly in front of the reader.

3) Using the handle, the reader sets the cup upright with the handle to his right. He then begins reading just to the left of the handle, moving left all the way around the cup.

4) The reader concentrates on the configuration of leaves as he ponders the questioner and his question. He studies the configurations and the symbols they depict. The handle and area directly to its left represent the questioner and his home. The further from the handle, the more distant the symbol is from the asker.

Symbols close to the handle show the immediate future. Symbols near the rim of the cup are further in the future. Symbols on the bottom of the cup represent the distant future. With experience, the reader can see symbols much as one can see pictures formed by clouds or by the embers of a fire.

5) The following are the meanings of various symbols:

- ♦ tree= growth...of a business, of a plan etc.
- ♦ bridge= new starts, new thinking
- ♦ leaves= changes for the better
- ♦ anchors= stability
- ♦ crown= a reward or distinction
- ♦ book= insight

- ladder= advancement
- cow= financial gain
- cloud= doubts
- rings= marriage
- eggs= luck changes for the better
- initials= significant others in the questioners life
- cat= treachery
- coffin= death
- hourglass= time is running out
- swords or guns= danger

When reading tea leaves, the reader looks for these symbols and their placement in proximity to the handle of the cup. As he begins to see symbols, he perceives his first impression as the answer to the question. Tea leaves must be read keeping in mind the question which was asked. Symbols must be interpreted in the context of the asker's life.

The best part of tea leaf reading: it's okay to read your own leaves. So study those leaves...have a ball!

JAPANESE TEA CEREMONY

From *Okakura Kakuzo's beautiful little book,* The Book of Tea *(see reference in Bibliography), we find the purpose behind the Japanese Ceremony:*

"Tea provides a situation, a quiet and peaceful environment for a man to meditate. Teaism is the discipline of the mind, body, heart and spirit. It is a cult founded on the adoration of the beautiful among the sordid facts of everyday existence. It inculcates purity and harmony, the mystery of mutual charity, the romanticism of the social order. It is essentially a worship of the imperfect, as it is a tender attempt to accomplish something possible in this impossible thing we know as life."

Volumes have been written about the Japanese Tea Ceremony which is actually an art form requiring years of study, practice and an artistic soul. The author recommends that the reader take part in an authentic Japanese Tea

Ceremony performed by a tea master. If the reader lives in a large city, a tea master may be available through a tea specialty store. In Cleveland, Ohio, for example, The Wabi Shop (see reference in "Mail Order"), has such a tea master who conducts a version of The Japanese Tea Ceremony as well as authentic Chinese Tea Ceremonies.

A JAPANESE TEA CELEBRATION

Although this author does not feel qualified or competent to write on the Japanese Tea Ceremony, she does feel most qualified to write about Japanese Tea Celebrations. Her celebration requires the most simplistic of foods, beautifully presented to good friends in a joyful atmosphere. The author recommends the use of Matcha or powdered green tea leaves although other high quality green teas could be used.

The preparations for the Japanese Tea Celebration can all be made in advance. They also provide for a lovely light lunch or for a delicious late afternoon energy boost.

CHICKEN SOUP (SUIMONO)

6 cups (1.5 liters) chicken stock (home-made or prepared)

2 medium leeks with greens, chopped (30 gm)

4 large mush-rooms, diced (15 gm)

1 carrot, peeled and diced (15 gm)

2 teaspoons (10 gm) soy sauce

1/4 cup (60 ml) saki

beautifully carved veg-etables such as carrot coins, mush-room crowns, scallion fans

Serve in beautiful Japanese tea bowls with ceramic spoons, if possible. It is most important to garnish this soup beautifully.

Serves: 6

In a large stock pot heat chicken stock. Add leeks, mushrooms, carrots, soy sauce and saki. Poach vegetables until just tender. The soup may be refrigerated at this point, and it keeps well. Heat gently, however, and do not boil. Garnish with reserved vegetables.

Each serving: 81 calories; 1% calories from fat; 2 gm total fat; less than 1 gm saturated fat; 00 mg cholesterol; 903* mg sodium; 00 mg caffeine.

*To reduce the high sodium content, use low sodium chicken stock and "lite" soy sauce.

RUMAKI

...a lightened version of the traditional Rumaki. Prepare these in advance and warm at the last minute or serve at room temperature.

Serves: 6, two-piece servings

In a shallow bowl, blend soy sauce with brown sugar, garlic and ginger. Wrap bacon around a piece of scallop and a pea pod. Secure with a toothpick. Marinate, refrigerated, for 4 hours or overnight in the soy mixture. Preheat oven to 400 degrees F (200 C). Arrange rumaki on a baking pan. Bake for 30 minutes, turning one time. Bacon should be crisp.

Each serving: 81 calories; 35% calories from fat; 3 gm total fat; 1 gm saturated fat; 12 mg cholesterol; 504 mg sodium; 00 mg caffeine.

1/4 cup (120 gm) soy sauce

2 tablespoons (30 gm) brown sugar

1 clove garlic, sliced

2 thin slices ginger

6 slices bacon, cut into 2 pieces

1/4 pound (120 gm) fresh scallops, cut into 12 pieces

12 pea pods

CUCUMBERS AND CHESTNUTS

1/4 cup (60 ml) vinegar

1 tablespoon (15 gm) sugar

1 teaspoon (5 gm) soy sauce

1 can, 4-1/2 ounces (135 gm) water chestnuts, drained

2 medium cucumbers, partially peeled, and sliced

lettuce leaves

pimento strips

1 tablespoon (15 gm) toasted sesame seeds

...a quick and easy salad-type appetizer.

Serves: 6

In a medium-sized mixing bowl, blend vinegar with sugar and soy sauce. Add water chestnuts and cucumber, stirring to coat. Allow to marinate for 1 hour.

To serve: place lettuce leaves onto a serving plate. Top with chestnuts and cucumber. Garnish with pimento strips and sesame seeds.

Each serving: 32 calories; 2% calories from fat; less than 1 gm total fat; 00 gm saturated fat; 00 mg cholesterol; 35 mg sodium; 00 mg caffeine.

GINGERED SHRIMP

Fresh shrimp is certainly far superior to the frozen variety. However, with the other fragrant ingredients, frozen shrimp will do just fine here.

Serves: 6

Heat water in a large soup pot. When water boils, drop in shrimp. It is very important to cook shrimp until they just turn red, about 1 to 2 minutes. Remove shrimp and immerse them in ice water for a couple of minutes to stop the cooking. Drain. Arrange shrimp in a medium sized baking dish. Heat soy sauce with ginger root, vinegar, sugar, sake and salt. When mixture boils, lower temperature and allow to cook for 5 minutes. Pour over shrimp. Cover and refrigerate for at least 1 hour.

To serve: drain shrimp and arrange on a serving plate. Garnish with chopped scallion.

Each serving: 59 calories; 1% calories from fat; less than 1 gm total fat; less than 1 gm saturated fat; 420 mg cholesterol; 00 mg sodium; 00 mg caffeine.

1/2 pound (120 gm) medium-sized frozen shrimp, defrosted and cleaned

2 tablespoons (30 gm) soy sauce

1 small ginger root, peeled and chopped

2 tablespoons (30 gm) vinegar

1 tablespoon (15 gm) sugar

2 tablespoons (30 gm) sake

1/2 teaspoon (3 gm) salt

2 tablespoons (30 gm) chopped green scallion

THICK TEA (MAT-CHA)

6 cups (1-1/2 liters) cold water

4 tablespoons (60 gm) powdered green Japanese Tea*

*Powdered Japanese green tea, Mat-cha, is available at many tea shops. Or grind an equal amount of green tea leaves in a mortal and pestle.

This tea is prepared, one cup at a time during the tea celebration.

Serves: 6

Heat water to a boil. Ladle 1/2 cup (125 ml) into a tea bowl. With a small whisk, whisk in tea for 5 to 10 seconds. Serve immediately.

Each serving: 5 calories; 00% calories from fat; 00 gm total fat; 00 gm saturated fat; 00 mg cholesterol; 00 mg sodium; 95 mg caffeine.

TSUJIURA (JAPANESE FORTUNE WAFERS)

This recipe makes up to 60 cookies. This is not a strongly scented cookie and complements celebrations well. I served these recently at the American Booksellers Association Convention in Chicago. With their very positive messages, these wafers were an instant favorite!

Serves: 30, two-cookie servings

In a large mixing bowl, cream butter until light and fluffy. Beat in sugar. Add egg and mix well. Stir in milk. Sift flour with baking powder and salt. Add to batter and stir until smooth. Add vanilla. Spread as thinly as possible on the bottoms of the pans. Bake for 8 to 10 minutes or until the wafers are lightly browned. Working quickly, cut into 3-1/2 inch squares. Fold over, stuffing a fortune into each. Fold and press the edges together firmly. If the wafers cool, reheat. This will make them pliable once again.

Each serving: 94 calories; 22% calories from fat; 2 gm total fat; 1 gm saturated fat; 13 mg cholesterol; 53 mg sodium; 00 mg caffeine.

non-stick cooking spray

1/3 cup (85 gm) butter

1-3/4 cups (420 gm) sugar

1 egg

1/4 cup (60 ml) milk

2 cups (500 gm) flour

1 teaspoon (5 gm) baking powder

1/4 teaspoon (1 gm) salt

1 teaspoon (5 gm) vanilla flavoring

60 written fortunes, cut into strips

ENGLISH BREAKFAST TEA CELEBRATION

It is said that during the eighteenth century, tea replaced ale as the breakfast beverage of choice in England. In fact, in England more than in any other country, specific times each day have been specified as tea times. Certain delectables and savories have been associated with these teas.

Breakfast is the opportunity to "break the fast", to celebrate the day and to enjoy hearty, delicious treats.

These recipes are meant to be served "family style". Or, dust off those snack sets, dress as in the "English Breakfast Tea" photograph ...and serve a blue plate special!

ENGLISH BREAKFAST TEA

English Breakfast Tea as sold in food stores is actually a blend of any kind of tea. Prepare this tea or try a Ceylon Tea, but be sure to follow Daniel Mantey's preparation suggestions in Chapter 2!

For the tea:

English Breakfast Tea and Ceylon Tea, brewed according to instructions in Chapter 2.

BELGIAN WAFFLES WITH CURRIED CHICKEN

1 package, 1/4 ounce (2 gm) yeast

1/2 cup (125 ml) very warm water

2 cups (500 gm) all purpose flour

1 teaspoon (5 gm) baking powder

1/3 cup (85 gm) brown sugar, packed

3/4 teaspoon (4 gm) salt

1 cup (250 ml) apple juice

2 eggs

2 tablespoons (30 gm) vegetable oil

non-stick cooking spray

2 cups (500 ml) water

Belgian Waffles...freeze beautifully. To re-heat: wrap in foil and place in a warm oven for 10 minutes.

Serves: 12

In a small bowl, blend yeast with very warm water. Allow to cure for 5 minutes. Preheat the waffle maker for 10 minutes. In a large bowl, blend flour with baking powder, brown sugar, and salt. Mix apple juice with eggs and peanut oil. Mix yeast with apple juice mixture and gently fold it into the flour. Allow to rise in a warm place for 15 minutes. Spray the grids of a Belgian Waffle maker with non-stick cooking spray. Just before baking waffles, add up to 2 cups (500 ml) more water to the batter and blend well. The batter should have the consistency of pancake batter. Place 1/2 (125 ml) cup waffle batter in each side of the waffle maker. Spread the mixture with a spatula so that it covers the waffle grid. Close lid of waffle maker and allow to bake until steam stops rising from the waffle maker. This will take 5 to 8 minutes. When the waffle maker is opened, the waffles should release easily. Serve on a large platter with corn bread triangles and Curried Chicken (page 151).

Each serving: 87 calories; 32% calories from fat; 3 gm total fat; less than 1 gm saturated fat; 36 mg cholesterol; 174 mg sodium; 00 mg caffeine.

CURRIED CHICKEN

Serves: 6

Heat oil in a large skillet. Brown chicken breasts over high heat until they are very well browned on all sides. This will take about 15 minutes. Add salt, onion and water, cover and cook for an additional 15 minutes, until chicken is no longer pink. Remove chicken from skillet and allow to cool, slightly. Stir sour cream, ginger and cumin into skillet stirring to blend. Remove bones and skin from chicken and cut into bite sized pieces. Add into curry sauce, stirring to heat and coat all sides of chicken.

To serve: pour chicken curry into a large serving bowl. Garnish with mango, lime, scallion, green pepper and pimento slices. Serve with a platter of Belgian waffles (page 150) and corn bread triangles.

Each serving, made with non-fat sour cream: 137 calories; 26% calories from fat; 4 gm total fat; 1 gm saturated fat; 46 mg cholesterol; 44 mg sodium; 00 mg caffeine.

2 tablespoons (30 gm) vegetable oil

6 chicken breasts with skin and bone, about 3 pounds (1500 gm)

1 teaspoon (5 gm) salt

1 medium onion, chopped

2 tablespoons (30 gm) water

1 cup (250 gm) sour cream

2 teaspoons (10 gm) curry powder

1/4 teaspoon (1 gm) ground ginger

1/4 teaspoon (1 gm) ground cumin

slices of mango, lime, scallion, green pepper and pimento for garnish

CORNBREAD TRIANGLES WITH HERBS

non-stick cooking spray

1 package, 1/4 ounce (2 gm) yeast

7/8 cup (220 gm) very warm water

1 cup (250 gm) all purpose flour

3/4 cup (185 gm) bread flour

1/2 cup (125 gm) yellow corn meal

4 tablespoons (60 gm) chopped fresh herbs (chives, cilantro, Italian parsley and/or basil)

1 tablespoon (15 gm) vegetable oil

1 teaspoon (5 gm) salt

1 tablespoon (15 gm) sugar

2 tablespoons (30 gm) melted butter

This bread may be made in an electric bread maker. Simply put all ingredients except yeast into the bread pan. Add yeast to the dispenser.

Serves: 6

Spray a 9x5x3 inch loaf pan with non-stick cooking spray. In a small bowl, blend yeast with water. Allow to cure for 5 minutes. In a large bowl, blend flours with corn meal, herbs, oil, salt and sugar. Using an electric mixer, if desired, beat yeast mixture into flour mixture. The batter will be smooth. Pour into prepared pan, cover with a wet towel and allow to rise for 15 minutes. Preheat oven to 375 degrees F (185 C). Place cornbread in the oven and bake for 35 to 40 minutes. Place on a cooling rack and allow to cool. To make cornbread trianges: preheat broiler. Slice cooled cornbread into 12 slices. Cut across bread to make triangles. Place on baking sheets and brush with melted butter. Broil until slightly browned and crunchy.

Each serving: 197 calories; 32% calories from fat; 7 gm total fat; 3 gm saturated fat; 10 mg cholesterol; 396 mg sodium; 00 mg caffeine.

Afternoon Tea

...the very ultimate in teas...pull all the stops. Invite 4 to 40 of your very favorite guests. Of course, the most honored guest is selected to pour your exquisite blend of Moroccan Mint Tea. Set your mind free to explore colors and flavors with flowers and food. Memorable!

Photo Credits

Tea set is Stieff "Williamsburg," c. 1965, provided by Joseph Davis Antiques, Lakewood, Ohio 44107. Tea cups c. 1920, Chinese, provided by Affordable Antiques, Lakewood, Ohio 44106. 3 Tier Candy Stand with English Trim by International Silver Company provided by Al's Pottery, Lyndhurst, Ohio 44124. International Silver Candlestick; also, silver platters, pearl handle knife and cut glass asparagus dish provided by Mary Ward.

Recipe Credits

Moroccan Mint Tea with Orange Blossoms, recipe page 73
Blueberry Tartlets, recipe page 163
Cucumbers and Caviar Bites, recipe page 161
Shrimp Puffs, recipe page 162
Poppyseed Wedges, recipe page 164
Egg Salad with Capers on Polenta, recipe page 190

CRANBERRY MINI MUFFINS

This muffin is packed with good things!

Serves: 24 mini muffins

Line 24 mini-muffin tins with non-stick mini-sized baking cups. Preheat oven to 400 degrees F (200 C). In a large bowl, blend together flour, baking soda, salt and sugar. In a small bowl, blend egg with oil, buttermilk and yogurt. Blend wet ingredients into dry ingredients until just blended. Fold in cranberries and nuts. Fill each muffin tin 3/4 full. Sprinkle with sugar. Bake for 10 to 12 minutes or until golden brown. Remove from pans and serve immediately or cool on racks. Store in a sealed container.

Each serving: 99 calories; 15% calories from fat; 2 gm total fat; less than 1 gm saturated fat; 9 mg cholesterol; 117 mg sodium; 00 mg caffeine.

3 cups (750 gm) all purpose flour

1/2 teaspoon (3 gm) baking soda

1 teaspoon (5 gm) salt

1/2 cup (125 gm) brown sugar

1 egg

1 tablespoon (15 gm) vegetable oil

1/4 cup (60 ml) buttermilk

1 cup (250 gm) non-fat yogurt

1 cup (250 gm) fresh or frozen cranberries

1/4 cup (60 gm) chopped walnuts, toasted

2 tablespoons (30 gm) sugar

NURSERY TEA CELEBRATION

"I'm a little teapot short and stout,
Here is my handle and here is my spout.
When I get all revved up hear me shout,
Just tip me over and pour me out."
                    —a traditional children's game

Nothing is more popular with children than tea. They love to make it, to drink it and to pretend with it. Traditionally, tea party time was a time when the English child gathered around the small table for milky cups of tea and biscuits. The recipes used here have great appeal for children... and author's daughter, the director of a large child development center, agrees.

Recipes were developed for the children at Detroit Avenue Child Development Center in Lakewood, Ohio. These were the favorites!

Cambric Tea: Cambric is a very weak tea. Prepare according to instructions in Chapter 2. Serve it warm with plenty of sugar and milk. See the following pages for more nursery tea favorites.

CINNAMON BEARS (TOAST)

Easy...and nothing is more popular with children than cinnamon toast!

Serves: 4

Preheat broiler. With a bear (or other shaped cookie cutter) cut the bread slices into shapes. Brush each bear with melted butter and place under broiler until beginning to brown. Remove bears from broiler and sprinkle with sugar and cinnamon. Return to heat until sugar just begins to crystallize.

4 slices firm white bread

2 teaspoons (10 gm) melted butter

2 teaspoons (10 gm) sugar

1/2 teaspoon (30 gm) cinnamon

Each serving: 111 calories; 16% calories from fat; 2 gm total fat; 1 gm saturated fat; 5 mg cholesterol; 173 mg sodium; 00 mg caffeine.

C OOKIE SMILE SNICKERDOODLES

non-stick cooking spray

1-1/2 cup (185 gm) all purpose flour, sifted

1/4 teaspoon (1 gm) salt

1 teaspoon (5 gm) baking soda

2 teaspoons (10 gm) cream of tartar

1/4 cup (60 gm) butter or margarine, softened

3/4 cups (185 gm) sugar

1/4 cup (60 gm) apple juice

Topping:
1 tablespoon (15 gm) sugar

1 teaspoon (5 gm) cinnamon

frosting tubes for making smiles

The author isn't sure which gives her more pleasure...listening to her 20 month old granddaughter, Laura, say "Snickerdoodles" or watching her eat them!

Serves: 36 small cookies

Spray a baking sheet with non-stick cooking spray. Preheat oven to 350 degrees F (175 C). In a large bowl, sift flour with salt, baking soda and cream of tartar. In a small bowl, cream butter until light then add sugar and apple juice gradually, creaming until fluffy. Beat creamed ingredients into dry ingredients and beat until just smooth. Mixture will be sticky. In a small bowl, blend sugar and cinnamon topping. Shape into 1 inch balls and roll in cinnamon sugar. Arrange 2 inches apart on prepared baking sheets. Bake for 18 to 20 minutes until lightly browned. Cool slightly, then remove from pan to a cooling rack. Cool completely. To serve: give each child a few snickerdoodles and a tube of prepared frosting. Allow the child to make faces and smiles on the cookies.

Each serving: 52 calories; 24% calories from fat; 1 gm total fat; 1 gm saturated fat; 3 mg cholesterol; 52 mg sodium; 00 mg caffeine.

I CED CHERRY SCONES

Make these in tiny sizes...children just love these healthy treats.

Serves: 24, tiny scones

Preheat oven to 400 degrees F (200 C). In a large bowl, combine flour with chopped cherries, sugar, baking powder, salt, baking soda, yogurt, butter and egg. Blend until the mixture holds together well. Put mixture on a pastry board that has been sprinkled lightly with flour. Knead dough lightly, about 1 minute. Divide into 24 portions. Flatten and form into 1 inch circles. Flatten to 3/4 inch thick. Brush tops with milk and sprinkle with sugar. Place the scones, 1 inch apart, on an ungreased baking sheet. Bake for 8 to 10 minutes or until the scones are golden brown. Remove from oven and cool slightly. Serve warm.

Each serving, made with non-fat yogurt: 95 calories; 23% calories from fat; 2 gm total fat; 1 gm saturated fat; 23 mg cholesterol; 130 mg sodium; 00 mg caffeine.

3 cups (750 gm) all purpose flour

1/2 cup (125 gm) fresh or canned, drained, sweet cherries, coarsely chopped

2 tablespoons (30 gm) sugar

1 tablespoon (15 gm) baking powder

1/2 teaspoon (3 gm) salt

1/2 teaspoon (3 gm) baking soda

1/2 cup (125 gm) yogurt, non-fat or regular

1/4 cup (60 gm) butter

2 eggs

2 tablespoons (30 ml) milk for brushing onto scones

2 tablespoons (30 gm) sugar

AFTERNOON TEA CELEBRATION

In the states, we refer to the very formal afternoon teas as "High Tea." Actually, the formal British tea evolved from a "Low Tea" which was served mid afternoon to the aristocrats. High tea was the small meal taken by the poor British workers...a simple pot of tea with a few left over scraps...just enough to tide these poor workers over to the next day. In England, and in France, as in many European countries, taking tea in the late afternoon is an on-going tradition.

The accompanying recipes offer a variety of tastes...sweet and savory to compliment the strong black tea. Afternoon teas can range from small, intimate and informal gatherings of two or three friends...to large, formal gatherings that last several hours. In large, formal gatherings, it's important that the hostess select several "honored guests" who will act as "tea pourers."

Each honored guest is positioned at an end of the elegantly attired dining table. The honored guest can either serve a variety of teas or each serve just one tea. Some hostesses even serve coffee!

If a large, formal afternoon tea is planned, try these recipes and add recipes of your choice from Chapter 7. The following recipes would serve a beautiful tea for six. Prepare a selection of teas such as China, India and, possibly, a flavored tea such as Moroccan Mint Tea with Orange Blossoms (page 73) according to instructions in Chapter 2. Serve hot with plenty of sugar, honey and milk. If serving in quantity, see directions for serving hot tea in quantities.

S MOKED TURKEY ON JICAMA CRUDITE WITH RASPBERRY & BACON CREAM CHEESE

1/4 cup (60 gm) cream cheese, non-fat or regular

2 tablespoons (30 gm) crumbled bacon

2 tablespoons (30 gm) raspberry jam

1 jicama, sliced and cut into 12 small rounds or squares

1/4 pound (125 gm) smoked turkey breast

Jicama is a perfect vegetable to use in crudite tea sandwiches. It has crunch, very mild flavor and it holds up well. These can be made as much as 4 hours in advance, covered well and refrigerated.

Serves: 12 sandwiches

In a small bowl, blend cream cheese with bacon and jam. Blend until very smooth. Coat jicama rounds with half the cream cheese mixture. Divide turkey between the jicama rounds. Top with dollops of the remaining cream cheese.

Each serving, made with non-fat cream cheese: 38 calories; 7% calories from fat; less than 1 gm total fat; less than 1 gm saturated fat; 8 mg cholesterol; 35 mg sodium; 00 mg caffeine.

CUCUMBER AND CAVIAR BITES

There are so many subtle flavors in this make-ahead recipe.

Serves: 24 caviar bites

Place cocktail rye bread on a serving tray. Top each with a rim of onion slice. Dip cucumber slices into French dressing and place, dressing side down, onto cocktail rye. Dress with 1/8 teaspoon (1/2 gm) caviar each, a caper or two, and a touch of the egg yolk. Cover well and refrigerate until serving.

Each serving: 32 calories; 27% calories from fat; 1 gm total fat; less than 1 gm saturated fat; 13 mg cholesterol; 72 mg sodium; 00 mg caffeine.

24 pieces cocktail rye bread

1 small onion, thinly sliced

2 small or 1 large cucumber, 24 slices

1/4 cup (60 gm) prepared or homemade French dressing

1 tablespoon (15 gm) red caviar

2 teaspoons (10 gm) capers

1 hard cooked egg yolk, riced

S HRIMP PUFFS

1 egg white

12 medium shrimp cooked and chopped

1/4 cup (125 gm) grated cheddar cheese

1/8 teaspoon (1/2 gm) salt

1/2 teaspoon (3 gm) paprika

1/2 cup (250 gm) mayonnaise, non-fat or regular

24 onion flavored melba rounds

paprika for garnish

Prepare these up to 1 hour in advance. Broil them just before serving.

Serves: 24 shrimp puffs

In a medium-sized bowl, whisk egg white until it is stiff. Fold in shrimp, cheese, salt, paprika and mayonnaise. Divide between melba rounds.

To serve: preheat broiler. Broil until the puffs are lightly browned. Sprinkle with a little extra paprika for garnish.

Each serving, made with non-fat mayonnaise: 20 calories; 36% calories from fat; 1 gm total fat; less than 1 gm saturated fat; 7 mg cholesterol; 42 mg sodium; 00 mg caffeine.

BLUEBERRY TARTLETS

When in a hurry, use premade tart shells.

Serves: 6

In a medium-sized bowl, blend flour with butter, sugar and salt. Blend with hands or a pastry cutter until mixture resembles coarse meal. Sprinkle with water and toss with a fork. Roll this into a ball, cover and refrigerate for 1 hour. Preheat oven to 350 degrees F (175 C). Divide pastry into 6 parts. Roll each into a thin tartlet shell and fit into a muffin tin. Bake for 10 minutes or until the pastry is golden brown. Wash and hull the blueberries. Remove 1/2 cup (125 gm) of the berries for puree. Puree these berries in a food processor or blender until smooth consistency. In a sauce pan, bring the blueberry puree and sugar to boil. Boil for 3 minutes until all sugar is dissolved. Remove from heat. Soften the gelatin in water, then blend with the hot blueberry puree. Beat with electric mixer or with a whisk until the gelatin and blueberry puree are smooth and thick. Divide remaining blueberries between tartlet shells. Carefully, pour hot puree over blueberries coating all fresh berries. Refrigerate for 4 hours before serving. Garnish with clotted cream.

Each serving: 110 calories; 39% calories from fat; 5 gm total fat; 7 gm saturated fat; 3 mg cholesterol; 13 mg sodium; 130 mg caffeine.

Tartlet crust:
3/4 cup (185 gm) all purpose flour

1/4 cup (60 gm) butter, chilled and cut into small pieces

1 tablespoon (15 gm) sugar

1/2 teaspoon (3 gm) salt

1/4 cup (60 ml) ice water

Filling:
2 cups (250 gm) blueberries

1/3 cup (80 gm) sugar

2 teaspoons (10 gm) unflavored gelatin

2 tablespoons (30 ml) water

2 tablespoons (30 ml) clotted cream (or Devonshire Cream)

POPPYSEED WEDGES

2 tablespoons
(30 gm) poppy
seeds

1 cup (250 ml)
boiling water

1-1/3 cups
(320 gm) all
purpose flour

1 teaspoon
(5 gm) baking
powder

1/2 teaspoon
(3 gm) baking
soda

1/2 teaspoon
(3 gm) salt

1/4 cup (60
gm) light
margarine

3/4 cup
(180 gm) sugar

1 teaspoon
(5 gm) vanilla

2 egg whites,
whip with fork

3/4 cups (180
gm) buttermilk

This is a light sweet cake that goes well with hot tea.

Serves: 8

Spray an 8x8 inch round pan with non-stick cooking spray. Preheat oven to 375 degrees F (185 C). Soak poppy seeds in 1 cup boiling water for 1 hour. Line a tea strainer with a paper towel and drain poppy seeds into it. In a medium sized bowl, combine flour with baking powder, baking soda and salt. In a large bowl, cream together margarine, sugar, and vanilla. Add eggs, creaming to a smooth mixture. Add dry ingredients to creamed mixture alternately with buttermilk. Fold in drained poppy seeds. Pour into prepared pan. Bake for 25 to 30 minutes until cake springs back when touched lightly in the center.

To serve: cut cake into 8 wedges.

Each serving: 188 calories; 16% calories from fat; 4 gm total fat; less than 1 gm saturated fat; less than 1 mg cholesterol; 329 mg sodium; 00 mg caffeine.

Orange Graniti

This Italian ice makes a nice appearance on the Afternoon Tea table. Frozen firmly, it will last for 30 minutes or more.

Serves: 6

1 cup (250 ml) freshly squeezed orange juice

1/3 cup (85 gm) sugar

2 cups (500 ml) water

1 egg white

mint leaves for garnish

In a small mixing bowl, blend juice with sugar and water. Allow to stand for 5 minutes to soften. Meanwhile, place egg white in a small bowl and whip with an electric mixer or by hand until soft peaks form. Clean beaters, and beat orange juice mixture until smooth and all sugar has been dissolved. Fold in egg white. Pour into shallow pans or ice cube trays without dividers. Freeze until firm, about 2 hours. Remove from freezer and scoop into 4 ounce (60 gm) decorative dessert dishes. Return to freezer until serving time. Just before serving, garnish with mint

Each serving: 62 calories; 00% calories from fat; 00 gm total fat; 00 gm saturated fat; 00 mg cholesterol; 10 mg sodium; 00 mg caffeine.

7

SAVORIES & DELECTABLES TO SERVE WITH TEA

Ethiopian Spiced Tea...

For afternoon or evening, let this deliciously fragrant and spicy tea set the standard for excellence in entertaining. Finish the Brown Sugar Tea Cake with a lattice of confectioners sugar icing...perfect.

Photo Credits

Tea pot, cup, and saucers by Matthew Yanchuck. Provided by Fiori-Omni Gallery, Cleveland, Ohio 44106.
Cowrie Nigerian necklace provided by Donna Morris.

Recipe Credits

Spiced Ethiopian Tea, recipe page 78
Brown Sugar Tea Cake, recipe page 175

SWEET DELECTABLES

Sweet delectables are delicious sweetly flavored foods that go well with tea. For a casual tea celebration, create several of these recipes, and see how beautiful a Sweet Delectable Tray can be.

B ANANA SWIRL TEA ROLLS

non-stick cooking spray

Roll mixture:
2 packages, 1/4 ounce (7 gm), dry yeast

1/2 cup (125 ml) very warm, 115 degree (60 C), water

1 cup (250 ml) milk, non-fat or regular

1/4 cup (60 gm) butter

1/2 cup (125 gm) sugar

1/2 cup (125 gm) sour cream

1 teaspoon salt (5 gm)

3 cups (750 gm) all purpose flour

cont. page 171

This recipe is one of the author's favorites. Each time she makes it, she changes it just a little. Make these large or make then tiny...they smell so fragrant while baking.

Serves: 36 Rolls

Spray a large bowl with non-stick cooking spray. Spray 2 baking sheets with non-stick cooking spray. In a small bowl, blend yeast with water. Allow to cure for 5 minutes. In a medium sized saucepan, combine milk with butter. Heat until very warm but not boiling. Pour into a large bowl. With an electric mixer, blend in sugar, sour cream, salt and 1 cup all purpose flour. Add egg, banana and yeast. Mix well.

Add remaining white and bread flour to make a soft dough. Continue blending until the dough is smooth and satiny; this will take about 5 minutes if using a mixer and 10 minutes if kneading by hand. Put dough in prepared bowl, turning it to coat all sides of dough. Cover with a damp towel and allow to rise in a warm, draft-free place until doubled, about 1 hour.   (cont. page 171)

Combine brown sugar with cinnamon and sliced almonds. Blend well. Knead down dough and divide into 2 parts. Allow to rest for 10 minutes. Preheat oven to 375 degrees F. (185 C).

On a floured surface, roll half the dough into a 15x10 inch rectangle. Spread with half the butter and half the cinnamon mixture. Starting at the long edge, roll dough as with a jelly roll. Slice into 1 inch pieces and put onto prepared pan. Repeat with remaining dough. Bake for 15 minutes or until lightly browned. Remove from oven and remove rolls to a cooling rack. Cool completely.

Combine confectioners sugar with milk and almond. Drizzle glaze over the rolls.

Each serving, made with non-fat milk and sour cream: 114 calories; 23% calories from fat; 3 gm total fat; 1 gm saturated fat; 10 mg cholesterol; 86 mg sodium; 00 mg caffeine.

1 egg

1 banana very ripe, mashed

1-1/2 cups (375 gm) bread flour

Filling:
1/2 cup (120 gm) brown sugar

1 teaspoon (5 gm) cinnamon

1/2 cup (125 gm) sliced almonds

1 tablespoon (15 gm) butter, melted

Glaze:
1 cup (250 gm) confectioners sugar

7 teaspoons (35 gm) milk

1/4 teaspoon (1 gm) almond extract

Brioche

non-stick
cooking spray

1 tablespoon
(15 gm) yeast

1 cup (25 ml)
milk, non-fat or
regular scalded
then cooled to
115 degrees F
(60 C)

3-1/2 to 4 cups
(400-500 gm)
all purpose
flour

1 cup (125 gm)
bread flour

1/4 cup (60 gm)
sugar

cont. page 173

Brioche is a little complicated, but from the dough can be made delicious Glazed Doughnuts, Brown Sugar Tea Cake and Danish Pastry. Make the full recipe here, then use 1/4 for Brioche, 1/4 for 6 Glazed Doughnuts, 1/4 for Brown Sugar Coffee Cake, and 1/4 for Danish Pastry.

Serves: 24 Brioches

Spray a large bowl with non-stick cooking spray. In a small bowl, blend yeast with milk and allow to cure for 5 minutes.

Blend 2-1/2 cups (375 gm) flour and 1 cup (125 gm) bread flour with sugar and salt in a large bowl. Pour yeast mixture over flour mixture and add butter and eggs. Blend to make a smooth dough. Turn onto a floured board and knead to incorporate only enough of the remaining flour to make a smooth and elastic dough. Place in prepared bowl and cover with plastic wrap and wet towel. Allow to rise in a warm, draft-free place until dough doubles in bulk, about 1 hour.

(con.t page 173)

Prepare 24 brioche pans or muffin tins by spraying with non-stick cooking spray. Divide dough into 24 balls. Divide the balls into 2 pieces, 1 large and 1 small. Put each large ball in a prepared pan or muffin tin or on a baking sheet. Flour your fingers, make an indentation in each ball, and put the small ball in the indentation. Cover and allow dough to rise in a warm, draft-free place for 30 to 40 minutes.

Preheat oven to 350 degrees F (175 C). Brush rolls with the egg white and sprinkle with sugar. Bake 10 to 15 minutes, until the rolls are golden brown.

Each serving: 135 calories; 15% calories from fat; 3 gm total fat; 1 gm saturated fat; 32mg cholesterol; 126 mg sodium; 00 mg caffeine.

1 teaspoon (5 gm) salt

1/2 cup (120 gm) soft butter

3 eggs

2 egg whites, beaten

additional sugar for sprinkling

GLAZED DOUGHNUTS

non-stick cooking spray

Whole recipe of brioche, page 172

Hot vegetable oil for frying

Feel free to form these into strips, doughnut holes, or rounds.

Serves: 24, one-doughnut serving

On a floured board, roll brioche dough to a thickness of 1/4 inch. Cut into 3 inch rounds with a 1 inch doughnut hole. Place on a baking sheet which has been sprayed with non-stick cooking spray. Cover and allow to rise in a warm, draft-free place for 1 hour. Heat vegetable oil in a large, heavy pan or in a deep fat fryer to 375 degrees F (140 C). Fry doughnuts and holes, a few at a time, 2 to 3 minutes per side. Make glaze by blending 1 cup (250 gm) confectioners sugar with 2 tablespoons (30 ml) milk and 1/2 teaspoon (1 gm) vanilla. Glaze warm doughnuts.

Each serving: 172 calories; 26% calories from fat; 5 gm total fat; 2 gm saturated fat; 32 mg cholesterol; 126 mg sodium; 00 mg caffeine.

BROWN SUGAR TEA CAKE

I love to serve this with Spiced Ethiopian Tea.

Serves: 8

Mix walnuts with brown sugar, cinnamon and raisins. On a floured board, roll 1/4 brioche recipe (page 172) into a rectangle 24x8 inches. Spread with nut filling. Roll, jelly roll style, into a 24x2 inch tube. Form dough into a circle and put, seam side down, on a baking sheet that has been sprayed with non-stick cooking spray. With scissors, make 12 slashes in the dough. Make a petal design by turning the flaps of dough alternatley inward and outward. Cover and allow to rise in a warm, draft-free place for 1 hour. Preheat oven to 350 degrees F (175 C). Brush dough with egg white and sprinkle with a little sugar. Bake for 35 minutes, until ring is nicely browned.

3/4 cup
(180 gm)
walnuts

1 cup
(125 gm)
packed brown
sugar

1 teaspoon
(5 gm) cinnamon

1 cup
(125 gm)
raisins

1/4 recipe of
brioche,
page 172

Each serving: 178 calories; 8% calories from fat; 1 gm total fat; 1 gm saturated fat; 16 mg cholesterol; 75 mg sodium; 00 mg caffeine.

Danish Pastry

1 cup (125 gm)
dried apricots

1/3 cup
(80 gm) sugar

1/4 (1 gm)
teaspoon
allspice

1/4 recipe of
brioche,
page 172

This easy-to-make recipe is very fragrant.

Serves: 16

Simmer dried apricots in just enough water to cover. Simmer until tender, about 30 minutes. Drain, cut up and mix with sugar and allspice. Roll 1/4 recipe brioche dough into a 16x16 inch square. Cut into 4x4 inch squares and place them 1/2 inches apart on an ungreased baking sheet. Top with a scant 2 teaspoons (10 gm) of filling. Bring 2 opposite corners to the center, pressing firmly to seal. Cover and allow to rise in a warm, draft-free place for 30 minutes. Preheat oven to 400 degrees F (200 C). Bake until deep golden brown, about 20 minutes. If desired, glaze with confectioners frosting (see Doughnut recipe).

Each serving: 110 calories; 8% calories from fat; 1 gm total fat; 1 gm saturated fat; 12 mg cholesterol; 49 mg sodium; 00 mg caffeine.

CHAMOMILE CRISPIES

...a delicious and crisp little cookie that is great with herbed teas.

Serves: 72 small cookies

Spray 2 baking sheets with non-stick cooking spray. Preheat oven to 350 degrees F (175 C). In a large bowl, sift flour with salt, baking soda and cream of tartar. In a small bowl, cream butter until light then add corn syrup, sugar and tea gradually, creaming until fluffy. Beat creamed ingredients into dry ingredients and beat until just smooth. Mixture will be sticky. In a small bowl, blend sugar and cinnamon topping. Shape into 1 inch balls and roll in cinnamon sugar. Arrange 2 inches apart on prepared baking sheets. Bake for 18 to 20 minutes until lightly browned. Cool slightly, then remove from pan to a cooling rack. Cool completely and store in an air-tight container.

Each serving: 29 calories; 9% calories from fat; 1 gm total fat; less than 1 gm saturated fat; 2 mg cholesterol; 26 mg sodium; less than 1 mg caffeine.

non-stick cooking spray

2-3/4 cup (640 gm) all purpose flour, sifted

1/4 teaspoon (1 gm) salt

1 teaspoon (5 gm) baking soda

2 teaspoons (10 gm) cream of tartar

1/4 cup (60 gm) butter or margarine, softened

1/4 cup (60 gm) corn syrup

1-1/2 (375 gm) cups sugar

1/4 cup (60 ml) cooled chamomile tea

Topping:
2 tablespoons (30 gm) sugar

2 teaspoons (10 gm) cinnamon

CREAM CHEESE TEA CAKE

non-stick
cooking spray

Dough:
2 tablespoons
(30 gm) yeast

1/2 cup
(125 gm) very
warm water

1 cup (250 ml)
milk, non-fat or
regular

1/2 cup
(125 gm) butter

1/2 cup
(125 gm) sugar

1 teaspoon
(5 gm) salt

1/2 cup (60 gm)
unsweetened
cocoa

5 to 5-1/2 (1375
gm) cups all
purpose flour

2 eggs

cont. page 179

*This cake is delicious and easy to eat.
This recipe makes 3 tea cakes. It's fun
to make one to serve at your tea party
and 2 to give away to your guests!*

Serves: 24

Spray three, 9-inch pie plates with
non-stick cooking spray. In a small
bowl, blend yeast with very warm
water. Allow to rest for 10 minutes. In
medium-sized saucepan, blend milk
with butter, sugar and salt. Heat to 135
degrees F (70 C), very hot but not
boiling. Pour into a large bowl. With
an electric mixer, beat in the cocoa
and 1 cup (250 gm) flour. Mix until
cocoa is well blended into the mixture.
Next, add 2 eggs and the yeast mixture. Finally, add remaining flour and
beat with a mixer or knead by hand
until dough is smooth and satiny. This
takes 5 to 8 minutes.

Spray a large bowl with non-stick
cooking spray. Place dough in the
bowl, cover and allow to rise in a
warm, draft-free place until doubled,
about 1 hour.   cont. page 179

Meanwhile, in a medium-sized mixing bowl, combine cream cheese, sugar, vanilla and egg. Mix until well blended. Refrigerate until ready to use.

Roll dough onto a lightly floured surface. Divide into 3 equal portions and let rest for 10 minutes. Roll each portion into a circle 12 inches in diameter. Place a circle of dough in each prepared pie tin. Spread 1/3 cream cheese filling in the bottom of each circle. Cut the dough that hangs over the edge at 1 inch intervals. Fold one piece over the first, continuing around the circle until all pieces are overlapped and folded over the filling. Allow to rise in a warm, draft free place until doubled, about 40 minutes.

Preheat oven to 350 degrees F (175 C). Bake for 25 minutes or until lightly browned. In a small bowl, blend confectioners sugar with milk and vanilla. When cake is cool, drizzle with glaze, sprinkle with almonds, and garnish with chocolate curls.

Each serving, made with non-fat milk: 214 calories; 21% calories from fat; 5 gm total fat; 2 gm saturated fat; 37 mg cholesterol; 136 mg sodium; less than 1 mg caffeine.

Filling:
1 package, 8 ounces (250 gm), cream cheese

1/2 cup (125 gm) sugar

1 teaspoon (5 gm) vanilla extract

1 egg, beaten

Glaze:
1 cup (250 gm) confectioners sugar

7 teaspoons (35 gm) milk

1/4 teaspoon (1 gm) vanilla extract

1/4 cup (60 gm) sliced almonds, toasted

chocolate curls

CREAM PUFF PASTRY

non-stick
cooking spray

1 cup (250 gm)
all purpose
flour

1/8 teaspoon
(1/2 gm) salt

1 tablespoon
(15 gm) sugar

1 cup (250 ml)
2% milk

1/4 cup (60 gm)
butter

5 eggs, room
temperature

If a pastry tube is used, the cream puffs may be made larger or small or elongated for eclairs. To make puff shells for crab puffs or other savories, eliminate sugar.

Serves: 24 cream puff shells

Spray a baking sheet with non-stick cooking spray. Preheat oven to 400 degrees F (200 C). In a large bowl, sift flour with salt and sugar. In a heavy pan, heat milk and butter. Add the flour and stir quickly with a wooden spoon. As the dough becomes smooth, stir briskly. When spoon leaves an indentation when pressed down on the dough, remove from heat. Allow dough to cool slightly. Add eggs, one at a time, beating well after each addition. Put dough into a large pastry tube (or form puffs with 2 spoons). Pump out rounds of dough for cream puffs or elongated shapes for eclairs. Bake for 10 minutes; reduce heat to 350 degrees F (175 C) and continue baking for 25 minutes until they are very dry and quite firm to the touch. Cool before filling. Store unfilled puff shells in air tight bags.

Each serving: 58 calories; 46% calories from fat; 3 gm total fat; 2 gm saturated fat; 50 mg cholesterol; 49 mg sodium; 00 mg caffeine.

CREAM PUFFS

Serves: 12

In a heavy pan, scald milk. Add vanilla bean and allow to cure. In the top of a double boiler, blend sugar with flour and eggs. Heat water in the bottom to a boil. Whisk sugar mixture until light. Strain in hot milk, continuing to whisk until mixture begins to thicken, about 5 minutes. Remove from heat, continuing to whisk until mixture starts to cool. Cool completely before filling cream puffs. Place cooled filling into a pastry bag. Make a tiny hole in each cream puff, and fill with 1/12 of the mixture. Serve immediately.

1-1/2 cups (360 ml) 2% milk

a vanilla bean

1/2 cup (125 gm) sugar

1/4 cup (60 gm) all purpose flour

4 eggs, room temperature

12 cream puff shells (see page 180)

Each serving: 138 calories; 35% calories from fat; 5 gm total fat; 3 gm saturated fat; 124 mg cholesterol; 85 mg sodium; 00 mg caffeine.

CRUMPETS

1/2 cup
(125 ml) water

3/4 cup (90 ml)
scalded milk,
non-fat or
regular

1 teaspoon
(5 gm) sugar

1/2 teaspoon
(3 gm) salt

2 tablespoons
(30 ml) very
warm water

1 tablespoon
(15 gm) yeast

2 cups (250 gm)
all purpose flour

3 tablespoons
(45 gm) soft-
ened butter

additional
butter for
griddle

Homemade crumpets are heavenly when they are fresh. These could be the basis for a lovely breakfast with friends.

Serves: 10

In a medium sized mixing bowl, combine 1/2 cup (125 ml) water with milk, sugar and salt. In a small bowl, blend warm water with yeast. Allow to cure for 5 minutes. Blend yeast mixture into milk mixture. Beat 1 cup (125 gm) flour into yeast mixture. Cover the bowl with a wet cloth, set in a warm place and allow to rise until doubled in bulk, about 1-1/2 hours. Beat in butter and remaining flour. Divide the mixture into 10 pieces. Place on a lightly floured board and form into 3 inches round. Place on a floured baking sheet, cover and allow to rise until doubled in bulk. Heat griddle. Loosen crumpets from baking sheet and place onto well-buttered griddle. Bake on griddle for a total of 10 minutes turning once.

Each serving: 133 calories; 24% calories from fat; 4 gm total fat; 2 gm saturated fat; 10 mg cholesterol; 152 mg sodium; 00 mg caffeine.

GINGERSNAPS

...so spicy and delicious with tea.

Serves: 48 cookies

Spray 2 baking sheets with non-stick cooking spray. Preheat oven to 350 degrees F (175 C). In a large bowl, cream butter with corn syrup, sugar, egg, molasses and vanilla. In a medium sized mixing bowl, blend flour with ginger, cinnamon, baking soda and salt. Blend dry ingredients into wet ingredients. Beat until smooth. Dough will be stiff. Pour a little sugar into a custard dish. Break off a small piece of dough about 1 inch in diameter. Roll in sugar and place on prepared baking sheets. Bake for 15 to 17 minutes. Cool, remove from baking sheet, and cool completely on a baking rack. Store any uneaten cookies in an air-tight container.

Each serving: 159 calories; 20% calories from fat; 4 gm total fat; 2 gm saturated fat; 34 mg cholesterol; 86 mg sodium; 00 mg caffeine.

non-stick cooking spray

1/4 cup (60 gm) butter or marga-rine, softened

1/4 cup (60 gm) corn syrup

1 cup (125 gm) sugar

1 egg

3 tablespoons (45 gm) molasses

1-1/2 tspns (8 gm) vanilla extract

2 cups (500 gm) all purpose flour

1 tablespoon (15 gm) grated fresh ginger or 1 tspn. (15 gm) ground

1 teaspoon (5 gm) cinnamon

2 teaspoons (10 gm) baking soda

1 teaspoon (5 gm) salt

sugar

GLAZED LEMON TEA CAKES

non-stick cooking spray

Crust:
1 cup (25 gm) flour

1/4 cup (60 gm) butter or margarine

1/3 cup (85 gm) corn syrup

1/4 cup (60 gm) confectioners sugar

Filling: 2 eggs

1 cup (250 gm) granulated sugar

1/2 teaspoon (3 gm) baking powder

1/4 teaspoon (1 gm) salt

juice of 2 lemons

Glaze: 1 cup (250 gm) confectioners sugar, sifted

16 thin slices unpeeled kiwi

Here is a delectable lemony cake with a delicious crust! Garnish with kiwi slices.

Serves: 16

Spray an 8x8x2 inch square baking pan with non-stick cooking spray. Preheat oven to 350 degrees F (175 C). Mix flour with butter, corn syrup and confectioners sugar. Press into prepared pan. Bake for 20 minutes until browned. Meanwhile, beat eggs with sugar, baking powder, salt and the juice from one lemon. Beat until light and fluffy. Pour over hot crust. Bake for 25 minutes until the cake springs back when touched in the center. Cool. Blend confectioners sugar with juice from second lemon. Glaze cooled bars. To serve, cut into 16 squares. Top each square with a kiwi slice.

Each serving: 159 calories; 20% calories from fat; 4 gm total fat; 2 gm saturated fat; 34 mg cholesterol; 86 mg sodium; 00 mg caffeine.

Gentleman's Library Tea

Gentlemen prefer tea! A tea ceremony for one offers the chance to gain new perspectives, new energy, and new direction. This tea is about function...pie charts and tea, contemplation for thee...the perfect escape.

Photo Credits

China is Rosenthal "Finestra" provided by Al's Pottery, Lyndhurst, Ohio 44124. Montblanc Rollerball Pen provided by Best & Company. Contemporary flatware provided by Mary Ward. Saddler Tea Pot, c. 1940, provided by Daniel Mantey, The Wabi Shop, Cleveland, Ohio 44106. In Daniel's own words, "I carried this Saddler pot on the back of my bicycle during one of my bicycling-buying trips through the mountains of Southern England."

Recipe Credit

Tea: a First Prize Flush Darjeeling, prepared according to directions in
    Chapter 2
Tomato Brushetta, see special directions on page 199

LEMON GRANITI

Lemon graniti is a nice complement to any black tea. It is pale and smooth.

Serves: 6

1/3 cup (85 ml) freshly squeezed lemon juice

1/3 cup (85 gm) sugar

2 cups (500 ml) water

1 egg white

thin strips of lemon for garnish

In a small mixing bowl, blend juice with sugar and water. Allow to stand for 5 minutes to soften. Meanwhile, place egg white in a small bowl and whip with an electric mixer or by hand until soft peaks form. Clean beaters, and beat lemon juice mixture until smooth and all sugar has been dissolved. Fold in egg white. Pour into shallow pans or ice cube trays without dividers. Freeze until firm, about 2 hours. Remove from freezer and scoop into 4 ounce (125 gm) decorative dessert dishes. Return to freezer until serving time. Garnish with strips of lemon peel.

Each serving: 47 calories; 00% calories from fat; 00 gm total fat; 00 gm saturated fat; 00 mg cholesterol; 00 mg sodium; 00 mg caffeine.

M ADELINES

non-stick cook-
ing spray

2 eggs

1 cup (250 gm)
sugar

1 cup (250 gm)
cake flour, sifted

3/4 cup (185 gm)
clarified butter*

1 tablespoon
(15 gm) rum or
brandy (or 1/2
teaspoon (3 gm)
rum extract)

1 teaspoon
(5 gm) vanilla
extract

*Melt 1 cup butter
over low heat.
Remove from heat
and allow to cool.
Pour off clear
butter allowing
sediments to
remain in pan.

...a taste from Proust's Remembrance.

Serves: 30 small cakes

Spray 30 mini muffin tins with non-stick cooking spray. Preheat oven to 350 degrees F (175 C). In the top of a double boiler over, but not in, boiling water, whisk together eggs and sugar. Whisk constantly until thick and creamy. Remove from heat and cool. When mixture has cooled, sift in cake flour. Blend in butter, rum and vanilla. Pour into prepared pans. Bake for 10 to 15 minutes until delicately brown. Cool and serve as part of an assortment of tea goodies.

Each serving: 75 calories; 59% calories from fat; 5 gm total fat; 3 gm saturated fat; 26 mg cholesterol; 51 mg sodium; 00 mg caffeine.

P ETIT FOURS

A tea would not be complete without these delicate little cakes. It's lots of fun to decorate them, and they add shape, color and texture to your tea goodies.

Serves: 36 Petit Fours

Spray a 9x13x3 inch pan with non-stick cooking spray. Preheat oven to 350 degrees F (175 C). In a large bowl, sift cake flour with baking powder and salt. Sift twice so that all ingredients are well blended and light. In a small bowl, cream butter with sugar then blend into dry alternately with milk and almond extract. In a medium sized bowl, whip egg whites with an electric mixer until they are frothy. Continue to whip until stiff peaks form. Fold into cake mixture. Pour cake into prepared pan and bake for 45 minutes.

Remove cake and cool thoroughly. Cut into small squares, rectangles, triangles and rounds. There should be 36 pieces. Place on a baking rack with a pan underneath.* (Cont. page 188)

non-stick cooking spray

1-3/4 cup (435 gm) cake flour

2 teaspoons (20 gm) baking powder

1/4 teaspoon (1 gm) salt

3/4 cup (185 gm) butter

1 cup (250 gm) sugar, sifted

1 cup milk

1/2 cup (125 gm) almond extract

cont. on page 188

3 egg whites

2-1/2 cups
(625 gm)
confectioners
sugar

4 to 5 table-
spoons
(75 ml) milk

food coloring

Blend confectioners sugar with milk so that the mixture is the consistency of buttermilk. Reserve 1/2 cup of the glaze. Glaze cakes with the remainder. Glaze several times so that the cakes are completely covered. Divide remainder of glaze into two or three different small bowls. Color with different colors of food color. Using a spoon and a toothpick, make flowers and other decorations on cakes.

*Glaze may be re-used. As it falls to the pan, remove with a spatula and beat with remaining glaze.

Each serving: 106 calories; 32% calories from fat; 4 gm total fat; 2 gm saturated fat; 10 mg cholesterol; 79 mg sodium; 00 mg caffeine.

SAVORIES

Savories are the saltier complement of Sweet Delectables. They are designed to add color, intense flavor and texture to a beautiful Tea Tray.

E GG SALAD WITH CAPERS ON POLENTA

...a very different and delicious "crust".

Serves: 18

1/4 cup (60 gm) onion, chopped

1 tablespoon (15 gm) extra virgin olive oil

1-1/2 cups (360 ml) chicken stock (homemade or prepared)

1 cup (240 ml) water

2/3 cup (170 gm) corn meal

1 tablespoon (15 gm) Parmesan cheese, grated

1/4 teaspoon (1 gm) salt

non-stick cooking spray

3 hard cooked eggs, chopped

1 teaspoon (5 gm) chopped pimento

2 tablespoons (30 gm) mayonnaise

1 teaspoon (5 gm) capers

Italian parsley

Line the bottom of a 9x9 inch square baking pan with aluminum foil. In a medium-sized saucepan, blend onion with olive oil. Over medium heat, sauté until onion is just tender. Add stock, water and corn meal. Heat to boiling, lower heat and simmer for 10 minutes. Add cheese and salt. Spread into the prepared pan and refrigerate for 2-3 hours until the polenta is very firm. Spray a baking sheet with non-stick cooking spray. Preheat oven to 425 degrees F (200 C). Remove foil from pan and cut into 9 squares. Cut squares into triangles. There will be 18. Place on prepared baking sheet making sure triangles do not touch. Bake on the bottom rack of the oven until browned on the bottom, about 15 minutes. Turn over and bake until polenta pieces are puffed and crispy. Meanwhile, blend eggs with pimentos, mayonnaise and capers. Spread a teaspoon full onto each toasted polenta. Garnish with a leaf of Italian parsley.

Each serving: 57 calories; 47% calories from fat; 3 gm total fat; 1 gm saturated fat; 37 mg cholesterol; 201 mg sodium; 00 mg caffeine.

CRAB PUFFS

These are delectable...make shells in advance: fill them just before serving.

Serves: 24

In a small bowl, beat whipping cream with an electric mixer. Add hot sauce and salt and beat until whipped cream forms stiff peaks. Fold in crab meat. Cut tops off the small cream puff shells. Fill, recap and garnish with caviar and basil leaves.

Each serving: 22 calories; 81% calories from fat; 2 gm total fat; 1 gm saturated fat; 12 mg cholesterol; 62 mg sodium; 00 mg caffeine.

1/2 cup (120 gm) whipping cream

a few drops hot pepper sauce

1/2 teaspoon (2 gm) salt

1/2 cup (120 gm) cooked crab meat or lobster meat

24 small, 1 inch cream puff shells (see recipe on page 180 but omit sugar)

red caviar

basil leaves

CRUSTINI WITH MARSCAPONE & PROSCIUTTO

1 small baguette

2 teaspoons
(10 gm) olive oil

1/2 cup (120 gm)
marscapone

2 ounces
(60 gm) thinly
sliced prosciutto
ham

24 pimento
strips for garnish

This is quite simple...if marscapone is not available, use creme fraiche, clotted cream or Devonshire cream.

Serves: 24

Preheat oven to 400 degrees F (200 C). Slice baguette into 24 very thin slices. Place on a baking sheet and brush with olive oil. Bake for 10 minutes until the crustini are very crisp. Spread with marscapone. Top with rolls of prosciutto. Garnish with a strip of pimento.

Each serving: 62 calories; 29% calories from fat; 2 gm total fat; 1 gm saturated fat; 7 mg cholesterol; 105 mg sodium; 00 mg caffeine.

S NOW PEAS WITH CHEESE AND HERBS

Beautiful color for the appetizer and tea sandwich tray.

Serves: 24 stuffed snow peas

Steam snow peas for 30 to 45 seconds until the bright green color "pops." Immerse in cold water and open each pod with the sharp tip of a knife. Blend cheese with red pepper. Using a pastry tube with a large tip, pipe cheese into each pea pod.

To serve: arrange on a serving platter with colored greens or intersperse on the tea sandwich tray.

Each serving: 16 calories; 52% calories from fat; 1 gm total fat; 1 gm saturated fat; 4 mg cholesterol; 19 mg sodium; 00 mg caffeine.

8 ounces (250 gm) snow peas

4 ounces (125 gm) smoked soft cheese such as Boursin (or Liptauer Cheese...see next recipe)

2 tablespoons (30 gm) very finely chopped red pepper

chopped fresh herbs

LIPTAUER CHEESE

2 packages, 6 ounces each (185 gm) cream cheese, non-fat or regular

3 tablespoons (45 gm) softened butter

3 minced scallions

1 tablespoon (15 gm) anchovy paste (optional)

2 teaspoons (10 gm) capers

a few drops hot pepper sauce

a few drops Worcestershire sauce

1/2 teaspoon (3 gm) caraway seeds

1 teaspoon (5 gm) paprika

Here's a dessert-type cheese that is savory and a great spread for crackers, vegetables or a good base for tea sandwiches.

Serves: about 32 two-cup servings

Blend all ingredients and press into a 2 cup cheese mold. Chill until ready to serve.

To serve: surround with a variety of crackers and vegetable crudités.

Each serving made with non-fat cream cheese: 12 calories; 57% calories from fat; 1 gm total fat; less than 1 gm saturated fat; 2 mg cholesterol; 28 mg sodium; 00 mg caffeine.

TARAMA WITH MINI CRUDITÉ & CRACKERS

Here's another spread...a staple throughout Greece. Here it's used as a spread for crackers or small vegetables. Although delicious, this recipe has very high fat content. The author recommends it be served with crisp low-fat water crackers, melba toast or vegetable crudité.

1 large potato, baked, peeled and riced

1/2 cup (125 ml) olive oil

1 jar, 2 ounces (60 gm) red caviar

1 tablespoon (15 gm) finely chopped onion

3 tablespoons (45 gm) freshly squeezed lemon juice

chopped mint for garnish

Blend potatoe with 2 tablespoons (30 gm) olive oil. Add caviar, onion and lemon juice. Beating constantly, add remaining olive oil a little at a time until it is all incorporated. Scoop into a 2 cup serving dish. Garnish with mint and refrigerate for at least 2 hours before serving.

To serve: place on a serving platter with crackers and small vegetable crudité.

Each serving: 29 calories; 85% calories from fat; 4 gm total fat; 1 gm saturated fat; 2 mg cholesterol; 28 mg sodium; 00 mg caffeine.

S PINACH AND HAM TARTLETS

Tartlet Crust:

3/4 cup (185 gm) all purpose flour

1/4 cup (60 gm) butter, chilled and cut into small pieces

1/2 teaspoon (3 gm) salt

1/4 cup (60 gm) ice water

Tartlet Filling:

3 cups (60 gm) spinach leaves

1 tablespoon (15 gm) butter

1/4 pound (60 gm) smoked ham chopped

2 eggs

3/4 cup (185 ml) milk

1/4 teaspoon (1 gm) salt

a few drops hot pepper sauce

2 tablespoons (30 gm) shredded cheddar cheese

Use tartlet pans or mini muffin tins for these dainty treats. Quick and easy: use prepared pastry crust.

Serves: 12

In a medium sized bowl, blend flour with butter and salt. Blend with hands or with a pastry cutter until the mixture resembles coarse meal. Sprinkle with water and toss with a fork. Roll this into a ball, cover and refrigerate for 1 hour. Preheat oven to 350 degrees F (175 C). Divide pastry into 12 parts. Roll each into a thin tartlet shell and fit into a tartlet pan or muffin tin. Bake for 10 minutes or until the pastry is golden brown. In a heavy skillet, sauté spinach in butter. Cook until spinach wilts. Continue cooking until spinach is dry. Divide spinach and ham between tartlet shells. Beat eggs with milk, salt and hot pepper sauce. Top ham with egg mixture and cheese. Return tartlets to the oven and bake for an additional 10 minutes.

Each serving made with skimmed milk: 91 calories; 49% calories from fat; 5 gm total fat; 3 gm saturated fat; 1 mg cholesterol; 107 mg sodium; 00 mg caffeine.

T EA EGGS

This tasty and easy-to-prepare recipe is just plain fun.

Serves: 12

Place eggs in a medium-sized saucepan. Cover with cold water. Bring to a near-boil, cover and allow to steep in the water for 15 minutes. Cool eggs (reserving water). Tap egg shells all over until egg is completely cracked. Return to pan and add salt, soy sauce, anise and tea to water. Heat to a boil, cover and remove from heat. Let eggs stay in water for 2 hours. Cool completely. When ready to serve, peel eggs and cut into quarters. Arrange on a serving platter with other tea sandwiches and crackers.

6 eggs
water to cover eggs
1 tablespoon (15 gm) salt
2 tablespoons (30 ml) soy sauce
1 whole anise
2 teaspoons (10 gm) Earl Grey tea

Each serving: 40 calories; 58% calories from fat; 3 gm total fat; 1 gm saturated fat; 107 mg cholesterol; 57 mg sodium; 8 mg caffeine.

DILLED GRAVLAX ON WHOLE WHEAT MELBA

Great for holiday tea parties, these tea sandwiches have such a festive appearance. Buy the best quality smoked salmon available.

Serves: 24 appetizer servings

1 whole wheat baguette, sliced very thin (48 rounds)

1 tablespoon (15 gm) olive oil (or a mixture of olive oil and hot oil)

1 tablespoon (15 gm) sesame seeds, toasted

8 ounce (250 gm) piece smoked salmon

8 ounces (250 ml) skimmed evaporated milk

1 teaspoon (5 gm) freshly squeezed lemon or orange juice

2 to 3 table-spoons (30 to 45 gm) horseradish

1 8-ounce (250 gm) package cream cheese, softened, non-fat or regular

1/4 cup (60 gm) fresh dill

fresh dill and chopped pimento

To make melba: preheat oven to 250 degrees F (125 C). Place baguette slices on a cookie sheet. Brush a tiny bit of oil onto each one. Sprinkle with sesame seeds. Bake for 1 hour. Store in a tightly sealed plastic bag. In a food processor fitted with steel blade, chop salmon fine (or chop fine by hand). Add milk in a steady stream until all is absorbed. Add lemon juice, horserad-ish, cream cheese and dill and blend until combined. Chill for at least 1 hour

To serve: Divide mixture among whole wheat rounds. Garnish with a little dill and pimiento.

Each serving made with non-fat cream cheese: 82 calories; 21% calories from fat; 2 gm total fat; less than 1 gm saturated fat; 6 mg cholesterol; 118 mg sodium; 00 mg caffeine.

SHRIMP ON BRUSHETTA

The brushetta makes an excellent "holder" for spreads.

Serves: 6

Preheat oven to 300 degrees F (150 C). Slice bread into 12 thick slices. Place on ungreased baking sheet and rub with garlic. Brush with olive oil. Bake for 45 minutes until very crisp.

Blend cream cheese with lemon juice and dill. Divide the mixture between bruschetta. Garnish with shrimp and dill. Serve immediately.

Tomato Brushetta: Prepare according to directions, replacing the shrimp with 1 cup chopped tomato which has been blended with 1 teaspoon salt.

Each serving: 125 calories; 114% calories from fat; 2 gm total fat; less than 1 gm saturated fat; 37 mg cholesterol; 184 mg sodium; 00 mg caffeine.

1 small baguette

2 cloves garlic, sliced

2 teaspoon (10 gm) olive oil

1/4 cup (125 gm) softened cream cheese, non-fat or regular

1 teaspoon (5 gm) freshly squeezed lemon juice

1 teaspoon (5 gm) chopped fresh dill

12 medium-sized shrimp, cleaned and cooked

dill sprigs for garnish

SPREADS

Nice for the tea tray are finger sandwiches with any of the following spreads. Use
seasoned melba rounds, bruschetta (previous
page), rye rounds, water crackers or good quality
firm bread which has been trimmed and cut into
shapes.

- 1/4 cup (125 gm) butter or softened cream
  blended with 2 tablespoons (30 gm) chopped
  parsley, dill, chives, basil, watercress or nastur-
  tium leaves

- 1/4 cup (125 gm) Parmesan, Roquefort or
  Romano cheese

- 1 tablespoon (30 gm) horseradish, chopped
  cooked bacon, anchovy paste, caviar or ground
  ham

- 1/4 cup (125 gm) chopped almonds or walnuts

To garnish these creations, use

- whole herb leaves of thyme, basil, oregano, dill, parsley or chives
- blossoms of chives, nasturtiums, or pansies
- slices of stuffed green olives, black olives, scallions, celery, radishes or carrots
- a few caviar, red or black
- small raspberries, strawberries or blueberries
- thin slices of orange, lime or lemon peel

To set up the tea tray: the author recommends using beautiful serving trays or serving plates. If serving plates are not beautiful, cover them with paper doilies of various sizes, shapes and colors. Next, when serving 12 people for tea, the author recommends 6 recipes...3 sweet delectable and 3 savory. Here are some colorful combinations:

TRADITIONAL TEA TRAY #1:
Mini Banana Swirl Tea Rolls, Chamomile Crispies, Madelines, Crab Puffs, Egg Salad on Polenta, Tea Eggs, Snow Peas

TRADITIONAL TEA TRAY #2
Tiny Doughnuts, Tiny Crumpets with Jam, Petit Fours, Lemon Bars, Spinach-Ham Tartlets, Shrimp on Brushetta, Garnish Tea Sandwiches

LOW FAT TEA TRAY
Frozen Lemon Graniti, Tiny Danish Pastries, Mini Crumpets with Jam, Shrimp on Brushetta, Dilled Gravlax on Melba, Tea Sandwiches made by substituting butter or cream cheese with non-fat cream cheese

INTERNATIONAL TEA TRAY
Brioche with honey butter, Crumpets with Jam, Mini Danish, Lemon Graniti, Madelines, Petit Fours, Curstini with Marscapone and Prosciutto, Tarama, Shrimp on Bruschetta, Dilled Gravlax on Melba

FRESH TEA TRAY
Glazed Lemon Bars, Orange Graniti (use recipe for lemon and substitute orange juice), Fresh Fruit such as strawberries, blueberries and raspberries

with a little marscapone or heavy cream, Snow Peas, Herbed Tea Sanwiches, Tarama with Vegetable Crudite

QUICK AND EASY TEA TRAY
Purchased mini muffins, Gingersnaps, Graniti (use recipe for lemon Graniti using any juice), any of the tea sandwiches, Tea Eggs, Liptauer Cheese garnished with herbs

B IBLIOGRAPHY

Blofield, John. *The Chinese Art of Tea*. Boston, Massachusetts: Shambhala, 1985.

Burgess, Anthony. *The Book of Tea*. Paris, France: Flammarion, 1992.

Calvert, Catherine. *Tea*. New York, New York: Clarkson N. Potter, Inc., 1986.

Campbell, Dawn L. *The Tea Book*. Gretma, Louisiana: Pelican Publishing Company, Inc., 1995.

Castleman, Michael. *The Healing Herbs: The Ultimate Guide to the Curative Power of Nature's Medicines*. Emmaus, Pennyslvania: Rodale Press, 1991.

Chow, Kit, and Kramer, Ione. 1990. San Francisco, California: *China Books and Periodicals*.

Franklin, Aubrey. *Teatime*. New York, New York: Fell Publishers, 1981.

Goodwin, Jason. *A Time for Tea: Travels through China and India in Search of Tea*. New York, New York: Alfred A. Knopf, 1991.

Grieve, Maude. *A Modern Herbal*. New York, New York: Dover Publications, Inc., 1982.

Griggs, Barbara. *Green Pharmacy: A History of Herbal Medicine*. New York, New York: Viking Press, 1981.

Kazuko, Okakura. *The Book of Tea*. Rutland, Vermont: Charles E. Tuttle Company, 1956.

Kowalchik, Clair and Hylton, William H., Eds. *Rodale's Illustrated Encyclopedia of Herbs*. Emmaus, Pennyslvania: Rodale Press, 1987.

Lust, John. *The Herb Book*. New York, New York: Bantam Books, 1974.

Manchester, Carole. *French Tea*. New York, New York: William Morrow and Company, Inc., 1993.

Marcin, Marietta Marshall. *The Herbal Tea Garden*. Pownal, Vermont: Storey Communications, 1993.

McCormick, Malachi. *A Decent Cup of Tea*. New York, New York: Clarkson N. Potter, Inc., 1991.

Ody, Penelope. *The Complete Medicinal Herbal*. London, England: Dorling Kindersley Limited, 1993.

Pratt, James Norwood. *The Tea Lover's Treasury*. San Francisco, California: 101 Productions, Cole Group, 1982.

The Republic of Tea, The Book of Tea & Herbs. Santa Rosa, California, 1993.

Stoddard, Alexandra. *Tea Celebrations, the Way to Serenity*. New York, New York: Avon Books, 1994.

Tierra, Michael. *The Way of Herbs*. New York, New York: Pocket Books, 1990.

Toomay, Mindy. *A Cozy Book of Herbal Teas*. Rocklin, California: Prima Publishing,1995.

Ukers, William H. *All About Tea*. Whitestone, New York: Tea & Coffee Trade Journal Co., 1935.

Ward, Mary. *The Top 100 Coffee Recipes*. Hollywood, Florida: Lifetime Publishers, 1992.

THE TOP 100 INTERNATIONAL COFFEE RECIPES

Mary Ward

How to Prepare, Serve and Experience Great Cups of Tasty & Healthy Coffee for All Occasions

In this beautifully full-colored illustrated book (the perfect gift) you will find one hundred recipes — and trade secrets — for creating the best-tasting, most relaxing and healthiest cup of "black gold."

- *COMPLETE NUTRITIONAL & CAFFEINE ANALYSIS ON ALL RECIPES*
- *CONTAINS A WORLD HISTORY OF THE RICH COFFEE TRADITION*
- *LEARN HOW TO BREW AND SERVE THE PERFECT CUP OF COFFEE*
- *ENJOY HOT COFFEES, ICED COFFEES OR FLAVOR YOUR COFFEE WITH SPIRITS*
- *DISCOVER THE UNIQUE TASTE OF ESPRESSO AND CAPPUCCINO*

★ **224 pages** ★**$14.95** ★**Paperback** ★**ISBN: 0-8119-0818-6**
★ **Contains 12 color photographs**

The Top 100 International Low-Fat Recipes
Cook Your Weight Off With Tasty and Easty-to-Prepare Dishes

Donald A. Kullman, M.D.
Nancy Szeman, R.D., C.D.E.

A comprehensive guide to preparing easy, delicious dishes that will help shed fat, lower cholesterol and keep you fit. Includes 300-food nutritional-counter, nutritional analysis of recipes and health tips.

★ *256 pages with 12 color photos* ★*$14.95*
★*Paperback* ★ *ISBN: 0-8119-0672-8*

The Top 100 Recipes for Diabetics
The Comprehensive Diabetic Cookbook — 3rd Edition

Dorothy Kaplan

If your doctor could cook, he or she would recommend you eat the healthy meals outlined here. This comprehensive diabetic cookbook (previous edition sold 60,000 copies) offers easy-to-prepare nutritionally-sound recipes.

★ *208 pages with 12 color photos* ★*$14.95*
★*Paperback* ★ *ISBN: 0-8119-0819-4*

INDEX

MAIL ORDER

The Daily Grind
P.O. Box 607
Nashville, IN 47448
812\988-4808

Grace Tea Co., Ltd.
50 West 17th Street
New York, NY 10011
212\255-2935

Nicholas Garden Nursery
(make your own tea bags)
1190 North Pacific Highway
Albany, OR 97321
541\928-9280
Fax: 541\967-8406

Simpson and Vail
P.O. Box 309
Pleasantville, NY 10570
914\747-1336
Fax: 914\741-6942

Uwajimaya
Sixth Avenue South and South
   King Street
Seattle, WA 98104
206\624-6248
Fax: 206\624-6915

The Wabi Shop
2017 Murray Hill
Cleveland, Ohio 44106
216\791-9224

Walnut Acres
P.O. Box 8
Penns Creek,. PA 17862
717\837-0601
Fax: 717\837-1146